Contents

Acknowledgements

It is with grateful thanks that I acknowledge Ruth, Ivan, Sacha, Martin, Adam, and my grandsons for love and inspiration, Warren Norwood for 'lighting the fire', Pam-el-La for belief, Evelynn and Leo for support, Krause Publications for faith, and the many readers of my first books for their wonderful response.

Milan

Preface

"I have my own antiques business."

That sentence opened a wonderful new chapter in so many people's lives that even I was surprised at the response. Letters poured in from all over the country as *Money from Antiques* hit the bookstores, and it was extremely gratifying to hear from so many people interested in turning their dreams into reality. Not only did ordinary people from all over the country take the plunge and start their own antique businesses, but many even succeeded in expanding from their initial modest investment. As Heather K. Harrington from Independence, Oregon wrote: "I am now even going to start buying antiques directly from Europe in April, 1998."

Three years later, I still have difficulty in grasping how rapidly the antiques business is

growing and what a financially rewarding and pleasurable endeavor it can really be. In just three short years, there has been a shakeout in the marginal antique malls, a tremendous growth in new, wonderfully innovative ones, the introduction of Internet selling and buying, and even a whole host of prime time antique television programs and syndicated newspaper columns that can be used to help you in your new business.

And what a great business it is. Not only that, it's all due to wonderful people like you.

Is the antiques business still as satisfying and rewarding as it was when I wrote *Money From Antiques*? Are the opportunities still there? Can one still succeed in this terrific business and make one's life both more rewarding and financially secure?

Of course you can. Just don't forget the following. Whether you are just getting started,

are already established, or are considering expanding, you can do it. You can succeed! Just remember what I said three years ago, give yourself a motto, write it down, look at it every day, and believe that you will achieve your dreams.

"How can I be so sure?" you may be asking.

As I said in *Money From Antiques*: "You as an individual have the capacity to dream and you have tremendously unique abilities." And now, by buying this and my previous book, you have the knowledge to start, the drive to expand, and even the confidence to become a major player in the antiques business in the new millennium. You are not alone. All my experience, knowledge, and advice is here to help you. I will guide you, advise you, and supply all the information you need in the chapters ahead to help you not only succeed, but to expand as well. The future is even more exciting than before. More disposable income, more customers, and new technology have made it so. Just don't forget what I said originally in *Money From Antiques*: "Nothing is set in concrete. Use what is applicable to you, discard what isn't, and above all else, have fun!"

So, let's get started and continue the antique adventure.

MORE MONEY
from *Antiques!*

〜 **Milan Vesely**

Published by

 **krause
publications**

700 E. State Street • Iola, WI 54990-0001
Telephone: 715/445-2214

Please call or write for our free catalog.
Our toll-free number to place an order or obtain a free catalog is 800-258-0929
or please use our regular business telephone 715-445-2214
for editorial comment and further information.

Library of Congress Catalog Number: 98-84443
ISBN: 0-87341-621-X

Printed in the United States of America

Chapter 1

*L*et's Get Reacquainted!

"I have my own antiques business."

What exciting words they were then, and what exciting words they still are today. When I first wrote those words three years ago, the antiques business was in an interesting stage of development. The advent of antique malls had enabled ordinary people to consider starting their own businesses, but advice and information as to how to go about it was sparse. Now, three years later, the antiques business has come of age and so many more dealers are involved that it's almost presumptuous to offer advice. In any village, in any town, and in any city, it seems that every large building is now an antique mall, and the antiques being sold in their booths are a wonder to behold. Furniture, accessories, posters, billboards, comic books and even dental instruments are now considered antiques. It seems that almost anything goes.

So has the momentum slowed?

Surprisingly, the answer is no!

"And why not?" you may well ask.

Well, that's the subject of this new book, and like before, I want you to remember who you are, because remembering who you are will enable you to meet the new challenges confronting the antiques business in the new millennium. And you know who you are, don't you? That's right! You are a wonderfully unique antique dealer, with all the attributes that make you and the antiques business such a special combination.

Enough of the chit chat. It is time for you and I to look back briefly, and then to go forward and confront the challenges facing both the beginning antiques dealer and the long established one.

A look back

First, like all prudent generals before a battle, let us look back and see what worked, what didn't, what has changed in the business, and how we can apply all the lessons learned. Let's also consider how we can use this knowledge and take advantage of the momentous changes now taking place in a business that has been, and still can be, so much fun. Once we've armed ourselves with knowledge of the new trends and factors currently influencing the antiques business, we can look ahead and achieve even greater results in the highly rewarding world of antiques.

So what went right?

$ \$ \$ \$ \$ \$ $

First of all, we chose the perfect location, didn't we? Of course we did. As detailed in *Money from Antiques*, we selected a great, centrally located mall. Using the guidelines I laid out, we opened a booth in a mall that was well organized, took care of the increasingly time consuming financial details, and expanded considerable effort to draw in the buying public. For those readers that took my advice—well done! For those that didn't—learn by your mistakes and don't give up. And for those new readers that are thinking of starting their own antique business, beg, borrow or buy *Money from Antiques* and look up the checklist in chapter two before starting. Come to think of it, I think I will too. One can never have enough knowledge of the basics that are so vital for success, and even I have forgotten some of them!

What else worked?

Looking back, my prediction on antique auctioneers was right. Many of the more shady ones have gone out of business. So have the marginal malls. But the economy stayed strong and new ones have sprung up. Many of them have the same problems. For both the established antique dealers and newcomers, I have the same advice. Do your homework and be flexible, flexible, and even more flexible. With a strong economy and more disposable income, the buying public has demanded quality above all else. Those that picked up on this trend, calculated their overheads correctly, and charged the right prices as I suggested, have flourished. For those readers thinking of starting, or just having entered the antiques business, I can't emphasize enough how vital it is to be absolutely ruthless in ensuring that your markup is correct and that you know exactly how much net profit you are making. Three years ago, three times the purchase price was a correct markup. Now five and six times is the absolute minimum, what with booth rental charges increasing, prices of good antiques rising, and the cost of advertising so much higher.

Enough of the past. Let's look to the future.

Looking to the future

There is a new climate in the antique business. Money is plentiful, the electronics age has overtaken us with tremendous rapidity, the buying public's taste has changed, and competition has increased.

But the biggest change has come in how antique malls have expanded and become far more professional. I applaud this, and I think you should too, for it gives a serious antique dealer even more of a professional base from which to start, or expand, an antique business.

Since this is the first chapter, I do not intend to describe the changes in great detail. That will be done in subsequent chapters. I will say that newcomers entering the business in 1998 will have to be far more professional than people entering the antique business three years ago. This is because antique malls now charge a whole host of new fees to cover their advertising, their increased overheads, their sales tax services, and even their store security services. Most, if not all, now deduct at least five to seven percent from your net sales for these services, and this fact alone makes your own calculations far more critical. But don't worry. The upside is that you get far more sales promotions to help you succeed and the antique buying public is far larger than it was two years ago.

$$\$ \ \$ \ \$ \ \$ \ \$$$

In subsequent chapters, we shall cover many other aspects vital to your success in the antique business. But before we do that, let us pause to reflect on a few things. To help us in this I have made a checklist. In the list I have elaborated on the various points to emphasize essential aspects. I have also covered a few points detailed in *Money From Antiques* as I consider them even more relevant today then they were three years ago. Just remember what I said then, and in the previous pages: You, as an individual, have tremendously unique abilities. Use what information applies to you in your own antique business, discard what doesn't, and have fun doing it, for without the fun your chances of success are diminished. Besides which, you're a fun person, right?

 **Checklist**

- ❒ Go for it--Whether you are just starting or whether you are expanding. Just don't forget slowly, slowly! More money has been lost in the first rush of excitement than I care to remember.
- ❒ Check your location carefully-- If you already have a booth it'll give you peace of mind. If you are starting out, it's vital. Check *Money from Antiques* for details. Location, location, location is the watchword for success.
- ❒ Be flexible--An open mind will help you succeed. By keeping an open mind, you can use what is relevant and discard what is not.
- ❒ Do your homework--Facts and figures are vital. Accounts are a medical checkup on the state of your business. More antique dealers go out of business because they don't take enough notice of the boring figures than for any other reason.
- ❒ Use all the resources available to you--They will help you in your decisions. Information is the lifeblood of the antiques

We are going to make even more money from antiques!

business, or any other business for that matter.

- ❐ Be ruthless with yourself--Not facing facts is the difference between making and losing money. You want to succeed, don't you? Facing the positive as well as negative aspects of your operations enables you to take advantage of the profit making aspects, while discarding the money losing ones.
- ❐ Be a professional--It's good for business. No one buys from the slouching, scruffily dressed dealer, do they? Customers expect you to act, dress, and behave like a professional.

In concluding this first chapter on our exciting journey into the antique business I would like to just go back to something I said in *Money from Antiques*. At that time, I said what I did to help you keep your focus and to strengthen your resolve you should get yourself a motto. The same holds true today—whether you are just starting out, or you are an old professional with two years in the business under your belt, or even if you are about to become a powerhouse dealer in importing antiques.

So how about this for a motto?

"We are going to make *More Money from Antiques!*"

Sounds good, doesn't it? Let's move on and have fun.

Chapter 2

What's New?

There is a positive climate in the antiques business today. The economy is strong, disposable income is up, and the buying public is confident, but cautious, of the future. All this helps the antique dealer. I personally believe that the conditions are the best that I have seen for some time, whether you intend to start an antiques business, or whether you intend to expand an existing one.

"But the general retail trade is down. How can it be good to start an antiques business in that type of climate?" I can hear some of my more doubting readers ask.

This is why: The antiques business flourishes when there is caution in the wind.

How can that be?

When people are hesitant about their future, they buy traditional, and what could be more traditional than antiques? Add to this the fact that there is a fair amount of money about in the economy, and that the antique buying public demands quality. Quality means better products, which means more pricey items, which in turn means more profits! Now can you follow my reasoning? After all, 20 percent of a sold, $500 antique Majolica fruit bowl is better then 20 percent of a sold, $100 antique red crystal vase, right?

Hooray! I hear you shout.

Not so fast. Just think of what I said.

Re-reading the above you will note I said a **sold** Majolica fruit bowl. Not only did I say sold, but I also said a **Majolica** bowl. This is where the professional antique dealer differs from the amateur and why success is the opposite side of defeat.

The difference is this: The professional will have done his/her homework. He/she will have read the latest magazines, listened to other dealers discuss what's selling, watched what customers are looking at, noted what items the bidding is heaviest on in auctions, and above all else listened to his/her customers.

Armed with all this knowledge, the professional dealer has been quietly buying up Majolica items (particularly the green and brown ones) and now that he/she has cornered the market in Majolica in his/her mall, this professional has priced them at a slightly higher markup than normal. In other words: the professional antique dealer has worked hard at keeping up with the new climate and trends in the antique business and taken financial advantage of them.

But all this information is useless if you are in a bad location or in a booth located in an antique mall that still hasn't realized that they are in the entertainment business as well as in the antique business. Let me give you an example of this. I heard a news item on restaurants that is applicable to us antique dealers. When asked what the secret of his success was in making Spago's restaurant in Beverly Hills so profitable, the owner said that he rated hospitality above food quality. Hospitality above food quality in a restaurant? Come on now!

As he said in his own words: "Customers know that my food is excellent, that's expected. But when my hospitality is exceptional, when they feel that they are special and that they are treated as individuals, then they feel appreciated and become loyal repeat customers. That's why I am in the hospitality business first, and the restaurant business second."

$ $ $ $ $

Let this be a lesson to us all.

On the same subject I remember my old insurance agent in Nairobi, Kenya. He used to keep a rolodex on his desk and check it every day. In all the years I did business with him, he never forgot to send me a birthday card. Not once! Not only that, his office was centrally located, the coffee was always the best quality and piping hot, and the magazines on the table were current issues. In other words he was conveniently situated, he made me feel special with the card, and he entertained me with great coffee and the latest magazines. I always bought my insurance coverage from him, particularly as he always gave me the latest discounts without my having to ask for them!

Trends

What will be the hot trends in 1999?

Accessory furniture is very popular. So are decorative accessories. Side tables, entry hall pedestals, mirrors (a perennial

Side tables, entry hall pedestals and mirrors are our favorites.

favorite) and small armoires are flying out the door. And for interesting reasons. The armoires are an example. Normally used
to store clothes, they are now increasingly being used to store
crockery and tableware in dining and living rooms. No longer
used just for clothes, they are now used for more visual purposes. Really pretty ones are being used as curio cabinets and display cases. Add a few shelves, keep the doors ajar, and voila! A
beautiful curio cabinet with your family photos wonderfully
presented!

You find that interesting?

Yes. So do I, particularly if you remember that two years
ago, armoires were being used as entertainment centers. Then
customers put TVs, VCRs and Nintendo games in them. What's
coming next. Computers? Why not? There's enough space in
most armoires!

This shows how fashions change and how fast we have to
pick up on them to keep abreast. But that's why we're professionals aren't we?

So what does this change in usage mean to you as a dealer?

You are going to buy only smaller armoires, right? Good. I
knew you were smart. Just stop for a moment and think about it.
Smaller armoires look more delicate and therefore, prettier. The

tall seven foot ones are too overpowering. Even more important is the fact that a shoulder high armoire can be used to display a nice flower arrangement on top—up there, behind that beautiful carved fascia. It makes the whole room look better!

Not only is a small armoire a beautiful display case, but it's also a decorative piece of furniture. Just imagine how pretty a shoulder-high pinewood armoire will look in a country-style kitchen and you will understand what I mean. Add some Blue Willow pattern plates, some Blue Willow cups, a Blue Willow patterned English tea pot, and you have a wonderfully cheerful setting.

Another reason why smaller furniture pieces are selling so well is that they fit easier in a modern home. Flower pedestals, mirrors, and accessory tables can go with almost all retail furniture, and even make the room less cold. So stock up with small accessory furniture, shoulder-high armoires and interesting mirrors, and then sell your heart out!

Colors are also important for an antique dealer. Burnt orange, deep blue, and blood red are the hot trendy colors! Orange and red in particular go well with the deep sheen of English oak woodgrain. Remember that, suggest it to your customer, and watch those shoulder high armoires and accessory tables sell like hotcakes. Your biggest problem will be to get enough stock to satisfy demand! Add orange and red Majolica and you will be vacationing in Paris later this year, I think.

Silverware and old varnished copper accessories are a hot trend.

Ah, well, I may as well give all my secrets away.

Silverware and old burnished copper accessories are another hot trend. This one will stay around for a long time because old copper and silverware has been hot for five years and supplies are difficult to find. If you're lucky and locate a source in some old barn deep in Wisconsin, buy the lot. You can't go wrong. Silverware and antique copper is definitely in. Not the garish, shiny copper, but the deep dark kind like a swarthy Mediterranean gentleman's skin.

Now that you have all those silverware and burnished copper antiques, what else are you going to do? That's right. You're going to increase your profit markup to take advantage of supply and demand right? Of course you are. You're a smart antique dealer after all!

Enough of trends. Just don't forget what I said before. By reading the latest fashion magazines and keeping your ears open to your customer's requests you can take advantage of trends and make **"more money from antiques!"** Using 'in' colors will also help your products move quicker!

Having all this merchandise is all very well if you are in a good location. If you are not, keeping up with the latest trends won't help you one iota. Don't forget, the antiques business requires a 'total' approach for best results.

$ $ $ $ $

So what's the latest in antique malls?

Looking back, everything I said would happen, has. Many malls have gone out of business, particularly those that mixed antiques with lower priced craft items. Why? Because crafts and antiques don't have the same customer base, that's why. Craft items, and I'm not knocking them, simply attract customers who want cheaper, cutesy things. Antique customers are more discerning and buy long term products. It's like that risqué and slightly crude T-shirt. It's fine while on vacation in Mexico where "I'm looking for a virile man," plastered all over your back is fun, but it looks very cheap at a barbecue party for your husband's boss back home. Just remember, antiques have a connotation with class, so don't mix them with cheap items in your booth. Or cutsey crafts. If you do, you're liable to find that nothing sells. The antiques buyer will get turned off because they are looking for something special and the craft or country item buyer will think that you must be expensive because you also sell classy antiques. That's a no win situation! Don't do it.

But that's exactly what some antique malls did and most are now out of business.

The good malls however, flourished. As I walk through many of the successful ones I am struck by how many activities they have going on, particularly on the weekends. Music, free coffee tasting, seminars on ruby glass, and a host of activities make good mall entertaining for the whole family. That's what made the difference. Shopping for antiques has become a pleasure for husbands and children, not just for mum, as the English would say.

These malls are the ones you want your booth to be in. Remember what I said in *Money from Antiques.* If the mall can get the customer in and hold them for a longer period, the more likelihood that they will buy—preferably from your booth—because you've also followed the same principle, and have an author signing his book in one corner to draw in the crowd! Nothing like a small crowd to draw in an even bigger crowd, is there?

One of the new developments in antique malls that I approve of is that many now hold their own auctions. This is a great trend! Not only does it give their own antique dealers an outlet for getting rid of slow moving stock, but it also draws in more customers and other dealers. Since 30 percent of the antique business is still done among dealers selling to each other this is a good thing.

I am so taken with this new development in antique malls, that I recommend that you get a booth in such a mall if you are just starting out, even if it's location isn't the best. And for those dealers that worry about walk-in customers competing against them at the auction—don't worry. Antiques are so individual that you might even be able to sell that accessory piece to go with the customer's bedroom suite. And if you do outbid the customer, they might even come back and buy the piece from you a few days later, after it's been nagging them that they didn't bid higher. Turning your money around for a small profit quickly is as good as making a bigger one over a longer period.

Market changes

As I mentioned in previous pages, the buying public is flush with money at the moment and it looks like it will continue into the new millennium. The reasons are varied, but the main one is that there is a sense of quiet but cautious confidence. So how does this make the antique business different from normal retail and are there lessons to be learned from this for newcomers and established dealers alike?

Well, the first thing to remember is that strong economic times are both good and bad for the antique business. "Good and bad?" I hear you ask puzzled. Yes, good and bad.

Good, because customers buy better quality products and spend more. Bad, because they also have more choices. It's like when you buy a new car. If your job is secure, you will add on all those accessories. If it isn't, you will get only the basic model. The same holds true in the antique business. Except that in the antique business, the good products are in limited supply. Everyone's after them, and not only are they in short supply, but you also have to pay more to purchase them. This makes it even more imperative to ensure that you are ruthlessly accurate in your costing.

With fewer good products, it becomes more difficult to fill your booth or store. Just don't do it with junk, that's all. Remember what I said in *Money from Antiques*, and decorate with flower arrangements, throws, mirrors, candles, etc. It is far better to have three good armoires that you can decorate and show off well, than it is to have six, three of which are junk, that detract from your good ones. Not only that, the cheaper junk ones will give customers an opportunity to bargain harder as they will use them as a basis to knock your price down. It is more difficult to bargain with a customer if three units are $500 each and three are $1000 each, than if you just have the three good ones displayed and are prepared to drop one $50 to satisfy the customer.

Getting started in today's market

The same basics in starting an antiques business apply today as they did three years ago.

I don't want to keep plugging *Money from Antiques*, but since this new book is a continuation of what I said then, I simply don't have time to reiterate everything again. So many changes have taken place in the antiques business—the Internet has become a major factor, antique malls have become more sophisticated, and antiques have even become retail items in department stores—that I simply don't have time to cover all the basics. So without plugging *Money from Antiques* too much, I would suggest that you beg, borrow or steal a copy. If you can't do any of the above I'm afraid that you will have to buy one from your local bookstore or from my publisher. Their address is on the inside cover.

I will, however, expound on a few points.

Getting started in an antiques business today will require more investment than two years ago. An investment of between five and fifteen thousand dollars is necessary in today's market. The reason is that since the market is demanding quality products, the old antiques in your grandmother's attic alone are not good enough to start a business anymore. That is unless she was rich and collected a roomful of antiques over many years.

$ $ $ $ $

Those old tapestries, collections of historic documents, and even that old rocking chair will do as fillers, but you will have to buy more expensive quality buffets, glassware, dining table units, and mirrors to have a chance in making a success of your new business.

Not only that, a computer is an essential tool in the antique business today and this will cost you a minimum of around $1500-2000 for one that will allow you to access the Internet. The upside is that with the addition of a good printer you will save on all your sales flyers, follow-up thank you letters, and even on your record keeping.

I do, however, have a suggestion for those starting out. It is a well kept secret among professional antique dealers.

Take a long weekend off.

What? I'm raring to go and all you can suggest is to laze around?

No, lazing around is not what I meant at all. In fact you will work very hard while you are taking a weekend off. Let me explain.

All professional antiques dealers keep in the forefront of their thoughts the maxim: Buy low, sell high.

So where do you buy low?

Well, first get yourself a map of the United States. Then look up the rural areas that surround the city you live in. Then mark down all the small Podunk towns deep in the surrounding farming country. Then you let your fingers do the walking and call up all the small town city halls and find out if they have market days, celebration fireman days, or even duck racing days. Ask the officials if they know of any barns full of antiques in their area. You'll be surprised how everybody knows everybody's business in small farming communities. If they can't help you immediately, ask them what is the name of the local breakfast hangout and call the owner. Do this for a dozen towns. Before you know it, you will have a list of six places, or people, from whom you can purchase a booth full of antiques.

Since they have nothing else to do on cold winter evenings out there in the country, those antiques will be in top shape.

Oh, and don't forget to ask them if there is a small bed and breakfast nearby. Not only will you have somewhere to stay, but you will also have a possible supplier of antique furniture. All bed and breakfasts have them. Just remember: Avoid the tourist towns. You're looking for slow, sleepy dormouse farming communities, not chic, touristy weekend places.

Here is an example of what I mean.

One year ago I was traveling to Wisconsin on business. The little town I was going to was 30 miles from the nearest airport. Hiring a car, I traveled on all the small country roads instead of on the main route. Deep in deer country, I saw a farm with 'Antiques' scrawled in freehand on the outside of a barn. With $1500 cash I bought a full booth of antiques and now I have a supplier for years to come. If that isn't an inspiration for you to get started, nothing is!

Just don't tell everyone where you get your lower priced, but great quality, antique products. You'll get killed in the rush on that small country road, believe me!

One other piece of advice I want to give those starting out. Just remember what makes a successful business. Location, location, location, is the name of the game! It is far better to pay more rent for a booth in a better mall than it is to pay half the amount and get buried in a sleepy location where the only customers are looking for an absolute bargain.

Modifying your existing business

My suggestion for those antique dealers wishing to modify their existing business is to add more smalls. In particular I would suggest that you add more 'country' style items such as antique butterchurns, old horse harnesses, old church windows, and even if you can find them, old lampstands. Now I'm not talking about old craft items. Just old antiques. With more money about, customers are using such farm type items to decorate their dens and their sun rooms. That old butterchurn looks just great with a terrific flower arrangement in it. Long bullrushes and sunflowers on long stems will do very nicely, thank you. One other thing. Repaint your booth more often. Color gives it a nice fresh look. One new trend that I have noticed, and which I like, is that some dealers are painting 'olde worlde' scenes on their walls. You like that idea? I do to. It distinguishes your booth. Just make sure that your friendly amateur artist is good at it or else your booth will look like a junk stall. When I talk about 'olde worlde' scenes, I mean those that have ladies in fine feathered hats and lace dresses walking down the street, old horse riding scenes, and my favorite, the hearth and roaring fire scene with a shaggy dog lying on a rug in front of it.

One other suggestion I have for established dealers is this. Add a curio case full of antique jewelry to your booth. Antique Victorian jewelry and perfume bottles are very hot at the moment. Up until now, some dealers just specialized in this. By adding a display in one corner, you will have more customers coming into your booth just to look at these ladies items, and once you get them in, you can sell them a furniture accessory as well.

Taking advantage of new opportunities

What a tremendous change has taken place in the antique business in just three short years!

Antiques on the Internet, weekend antique shows in amusement parks, more and more antique newsletters, and a whole host of new weekend outlets have opened up in the last three years. Many of these are so important to today's dealer that I devote considerable space to them in later chapters. In this small section I would, however, like to remind you of some basics and the most important of these is: Keep an open mind, and consider anything that can be of help to you in increasing interest and therefore, sales. Just don't get carried away with everything you see or hear without evaluating it thoroughly first.

The biggest recent change in the antiques business has come with the use of computers.

Unfortunately, as we get older, we all tend to get a little stuck in our ways. "I don't understand those electronic gadgets," older folk will say. "How can I buy and sell on the Internet when I don't even know how to turn a computer on, let alone log on to a provider?" The excuses from dealers afraid of technology are many.

Just remember this: There is a ton of help out there and you don't have to be an expert in DOS to use a computer today. Just go to a computer store and ask them to show you how to do exactly what you want. Forget all the bells and whistles. Learn the basics for what you need, and you'll find it such a help in your antique business that you'll wonder how on earth you ever did without a computer before. In later chapters, we will discuss this in greater

The antique business is a home decorating business.

detail. Here I will say the following as encouragement: Just act like a child. They take to computers so well because they are not scared of messing something up. Children just go ahead and press differ-ent keys, knowing that they can't blow anything up.

New location criteria

Although I covered this earlier, I have added this section to cover one specific trend in the antique business. It is vital for both established dealers and those just starting out. This trend started

Country scene pictures sell well as do flower paintings.

in Japan and like many successful ideas it is spreading to the United States. I am already seeing it catching on like wildfire.

Antiques are beginning to enter the large department stores. And this covers both genuine antiques and reproduction furniture. Many department stores will soon have their own antique departments, operated by their own staff, or by sub-contractors.

The entry of such big league and deep pocketed players into the antique business will bring fierce competition—or increased opportunities—depending on how you look at it. For you who are get up and go types—get involved. Visit the store managers, offer to supply your expertise and accessories, and even offer your knowledge to help with their customer inquiries. After all, six-dollar-an-hour sales clerks don't have anywhere as much knowledge about antiques as you have, do they? For those of you that don't want to get involved in this new trend—watch what these stores buy and follow their lead. If they are stocking up on antique beds, you follow suit. After all, they have far more resources than you can muster on your own. My advice is: Use their resources to keep up with what's hot and what's not, just as I did by watching Pier 1 and the Bombay Company, both great accessory stores. When they stocked up on reproduction bedside tables, I followed suit with genuine antiques. Use their market research to help yourself. It only requires a visit to their stores once a month.

Which brings me to the next subject.

Broadening your antiques business

This subject will be fun for both of us. Don't you like it when business is fun? I know I do.

Three years ago I constantly emphasized that the antiques business is really a home decorating business. **This is even more true today than it was then.**

With this in mind, also remember what else I said then. I said that the percentage of people interested in buying antiques is relatively small, but the percentage of people interested in decorating their homes is almost 70 percent of the population.

Just don't restrict yourself. Broaden your customer base, and therefore, broaden your antique business by becoming interior decorators as well as antique dealers.

Here's what to do.

Add more 'country' style products. I've already mentioned old butterchurns. The old hand-turned ice cream churns also sell well. Horse harnesses are excellent for decorating dad's study. Old scythes and farming implements are often used to decorate sun rooms. Just add a sheaf of preserved wheat stalks sprayed with clear lacquer and you have a wonderful decorative addition to a 'country' style breakfast room. Which means that you will also carry a sheaf of preserved wheat stalks for sale among your display of antique milk churns in your booth, won't you?

Country scene pictures sell well, as do flower paintings. Oils are best, but water colors are also popular, particularly with rustic, distressed looking frames. I've also seen strange out-of-the-ordinary items like metal antique wash sinks—the ones your grandmother used by the outhouse to wash laundry in—used to hold flower arrangements in the most elegant of entry halls.

You've got the picture now, don't you?

Good! I knew that you would pick up on the fact that you should expand the amount of antique decorating items in your booth. This will become at least 60 percent of your business in 1998 and beyond, believe me.

Another strong trend emerging is decorating with Africana

items. Just don't forget that the African-American market is huge and that you should cater to it. Unfortunately, these products are more difficult to stock, but by hunting the Internet and the yellow pages you will be able to find suppliers. I would, however, caution you to use your imagination. Those wooden Kenyan giraffes are everywhere and are not antiques. It's better to have a few genuine African pieces than a lot of fakes. To show you that I follow my own advice, I will mention that in my living room, I have two carved Ugandan face masks that go terrifically well with the antique Scottish oak mirror and the antique pendulum clock. (see photo).

So broaden your antique business—add country style antiques, antique jewelry, and even African items. Just make sure that you showcase them well and that you don't just throw them in a pile in the corner like an afterthought!

New Products

Accessories are vital to your antique business' health. And they needn't be antiques.

Go into Pier 1, The Bombay Company, and any one of the myriad of accessory stores that are springing up, and follow their ideas. Just don't add the art deco products. They don't really go with antiques, even though art deco sideboards are still good sellers in the furniture line. Add the antique looking Tiffany lamps, the old picture frames and the latest candle lines. These may not be antiques, but they go with antiques and every add-on item that you sell with that gorgeous looking armoire or that carved English buffet will make your cash register ring. Mind you, I'm talking about accessories only not being genuine antiques, not the furniture.

If you can find antique accessories, even better. Old windowsill flower holders—the antique, rustic metal ones. Antique jars, antique foot scrapers, fireside scrapers, old model locomotives in glass and wooden display cases (you'll sell these for a real bundle) and those antique Dutch dog carts that are still around.

Here I must tell you an interesting story.

A friend of mine was on an antique buying trip in England and saw a really ratty wall-hanging bathroom cabinet. Its paint was peeling, the hinges were hanging on by a prayer and the glass was all smoky. Next to it was a four foot high bamboo trellis all covered with grease and grime. "I'll take them both," she told the seller, much to my amusement. "Just you wait and see," she told me defiantly, seeing the questioning look in my eyes. All I could think of was the embarrassment as we took them through the airport.

Guess what items sold first once she got back home? You guessed right! The greasy, grungy trellis and the battered looking bathroom shaving cabinet! I asked her why.

"Because people use them as decorating accent pieces," she said. "They will hang the bathroom cabinet up with a flower display attached, set the trellis in an entry hall, add a floral arrangement, and drape vines over them—the whole effect will be very chic!"

It just goes to show. There's no accounting for taste.

So what do I mean by new products? Anything that is interesting, old, unusual, odd, greasy, grundgy, pretty and even sometimes broken. Just remember to keep an open mind.

As the man said— "If you build it they will come." Which translated into antique language means— "If you get it, they will buy."

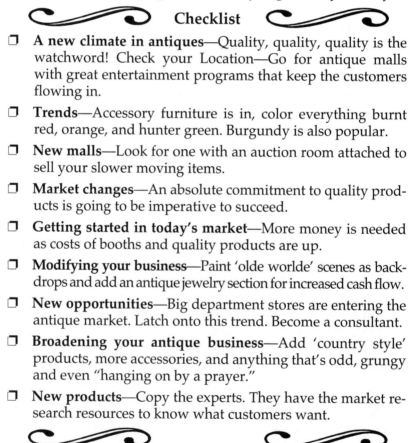

Checklist

❏ **A new climate in antiques**—Quality, quality, quality is the watchword! Check your Location—Go for antique malls with great entertainment programs that keep the customers flowing in.

❏ **Trends**—Accessory furniture is in, color everything burnt red, orange, and hunter green. Burgundy is also popular.

❏ **New malls**—Look for one with an auction room attached to sell your slower moving items.

❏ **Market changes**—An absolute commitment to quality products is going to be imperative to succeed.

❏ **Getting started in today's market**—More money is needed as costs of booths and quality products are up.

❏ **Modifying your business**—Paint 'olde worlde' scenes as backdrops and add an antique jewelry section for increased cash flow.

❏ **New opportunities**—Big department stores are entering the antique market. Latch onto this trend. Become a consultant.

❏ **Broadening your antique business**—Add 'country style' products, more accessories, and anything that's odd, grungy and even "hanging on by a prayer."

❏ **New products**—Copy the experts. They have the market research resources to know what customers want.

Chapter 3

U pdating Your Antiques Business

Those already established in the antiques business know that to be successful you have to be on top of things. Constant updating by repainting your booth, changing out your inventory, adding fast selling accessories, and keeping up with trends are extremely important chores. They have a direct effect on your sales, and therefore, on your profit.

So how do you keep up with all this work without beating yourself to death?

By setting up a program of change and by computerizing, that's how.

Before we cover the above, let's consider what updating your business really means. It certainly doesn't mean throwing away everything that has been successful to date. Nor does it mean changing your whole product line. What updating really means is taking what is successful, presenting it in new and interesting ways, fine tuning your display, and adding enough new products to make the whole booth look exciting and different.

The problem with all that—is that it takes time.

Not if you are organized, it doesn't.

So how do you get organized? Like all of us, me included, I am sure you hate paperwork.

To help yourself, get a good organizer. One of those with lots of writing space under each date. Either that or use the one in your computer. If you haven't got one, just go and buy the software and download it by following the instructions.

Now study the different sections of your antique booth, decide what products have been selling well, and identify each section by a specific name or area. In your organizer, electronic

Remember that lattice work you have in the shed?

or otherwise, make a note to change that section out next week and then make a notation to do the same again in three months time. Do this for each section of your booth. Start with the second section the second week. And so on, and so forth.

Once you have laid out this plan in your organizer, I suggest that you take a look at your booth as a whole. Use your imagination. Remember that lattice work that you have in the storage shed? How about repainting it, attaching some vines to it, and then using it as a section divider for this month's feature? And that old wine barrel? How about using it as a central stand for next months featured antique punch bowl? And that writing desk that is tucked away in the far right corner? Change it out with the wine barrel after 4 weeks, polish it, load it with men's gifts, and you will have customers commenting on how you always seem to have new products and how interesting your booth always is. Change is good in the antique business and also good for the soul! Okay, okay, so it's a little bit of trickery, but so what? You'll be surprised how that antique shaving kit that never seemed to sell flies out the door when displayed prominently on the writing desk instead of being hidden away at the back.

So what does updating your operation mean? It means scheduling change in one section of your booth at a time **on a regular basis.**

That way, it doesn't become too much at one time, only

takes up two hours a week, and always makes your antique booth an interesting place to visit. It also persuades a customer to make up their mind about purchasing that item over which they have been dithering. You'll be surprised how quickly a customer takes out their purse when the silver teapot that she's been eyeing is no longer in its regular place. She's been procrastinating for weeks, but as soon as you move it, the lady will buy immediately—guaranteed!

Learning from the past

When looking for ways to freshen your booth, I suggest that you learn from what has been successful in the past. Remember how that mirror sold once you draped an artificial vine around it? I bet you haven't been as diligent about your displays as you were when you first started your booth. It's completely natural. We all get complacent when things are going well. Just don't get too complacent or else you'll suddenly find your sales dropping. Just take a cue from one of the most successful retailers of all time—Wal-Mart.

Watch the displays in your local Wal-Mart over a period of a few months to get the idea. You will see that they change out inventory in one section almost every week, display the new

When looking to freshen your booth, I suggest that you learn from what has been successful in the past.

lines as if they are really hot sellers, and send what's left to another store. If you have two booths, you can do exactly the same with your inventory by alternating it between the two locations.

One more thing. If you look back in your records, you will note that old bibles sold really well in November. They were slow in June, however. Why do you think that is? Can it have something to do with Christmas coming? You didn't keep a record so you didn't pick up on this? Shame on you. Now you know why it's so important to maintain a record of such details.

Maintaining details is what makes a computer almost an essential tool for today's antique business. Whether you have one booth, two, or half a dozen, the computer is the most valuable tool in running your business professionally that I know of. Inventory control, pricing, change-out routines, costing formulas and a whole host of operational details become a cinch on one of these new-fangled things! And a relatively simple one costs well below a thousand dollars new, and half that used. Get one, use it and your business will benefit greatly. In later chapters I will even tell you how to buy and sell on them. Terrific thought, isn't it?

Coping with changes

Coping with changes becomes easier if you anticipate them. By reading fashion magazines, keeping your ears open during

Remember that punch bowl we used as a centerpiece?

antique auctions, listening to customer praise or complaints and visiting other malls to pick up ideas, you will be able to pick up on trends affecting your antique business. Just remember that you need to stock pine furniture at the start of the trend coming back around, not when the bubble has already burst for that year. The only way you can do this is to pick up on the fact that pine furniture is in short supply, indicating that demand and prices will rise in the coming months.

One of the major changes in the antique business in the last three years is that trends are coming around with increasing frequency. Pine, oak, mahogany, or walnut furniture is dropping out of fashion and coming back in with increasing frequency. It must be due to the increasing level of disposable income most people now have. When there's money in their pocket, they change out their furniture more often.

Coping with changes simply means being on the ball and keeping your eyes and ears open, right? You knew that of course. Oh, I forgot, you're an expert now.

New marketing techniques

Wow! Is this an important section or what?

New marketing techniques are as important to a one-booth antique business as they are to a multi-national corporation. By new marketing techniques, I mean presentation of product, attracting and holding your customer's attention, and new methods of building a larger customer base. Sound too high flying for a small antique business? Not at all. Just remember the old adage: You're in business first and in the antique business second.

So what does new marketing mean to you, the small antique dealer? To review, it means presenting your products in a new way, attracting a customer's attention, and building a larger customer base in the same way as larger retail businesses do. The principle is the same.

The best way I can describe what I mean by new marketing techniques is to give you examples. Let's take 'presenting your products in a new way' first.

Remember that punch bowl that we used as a centerpiece on that wine barrel? Well instead of just standing it on the barrel why don't we put it on an antique tablecloth, stand a bottle of White Zinfandel next to it, and arrange the antique napkins in their antique silver napkin holders around it? Having done that, drape a burgundy and gold ribbon in between them to tie the whole arrangement together. Sound good?

"That's just presentation," I hear skeptics grumble.

Not if you also write out a history of the bowl in calligraphy, call the whole package, "The Royal Collection," and offer the wine as a free sales incentive with the whole ensemble. Pack everything into a paisley patterned box, charge twice the price for "The Royal Collection" and start making up another gift presentation for the customer's friend.

That's called new marketing techniques. It combines "presenting your products in a new way (combination), with attracting a customer's attention (The Royal Collection), and building a larger customer base (her friend)."

And what's more, you can expand this marketing even further by asking Mary-Jane with the booth next door if she will consign you her crystal decanter. It goes well with the bowl. And while you are about it, don't forget to discuss that 10 percent commission she will give you if you sell it. Maybe even get it in writing?

New marketing techniques—they really mean new ideas of selling.

$ $ $ $ $

Here's another one. How about $10 gift certificates?

Print them up on your new computer, put a small notice in the local newspaper and give 50 of them away to the first 50 customers that bring the advertisement to your booth on Saturday. You'll be surprised how the little old ladies love them and the extra 20 sales will more than make up the cost of your "promotion."

Then there's two for the price of one. Remember those silver spoons that haven't moved for three months? Stick a notice up advertising a "two for one" sale at the entrance to your booth and watch them go!

Just make sure that you marked the price up 50% before you put the sign up.

Another new marketing technique that adventurous antique dealers are using is what I call the "Open House Technique."

This requires you to drive around your neighborhood, note which smart houses are for sale, call up the realtor selling them, and offer to supply that antique writing cabinet at a discounted price to any customer that buys the house. Ten to one the realtor will offer to pay for the writing desk if you display it in the house with a notice stating that it comes free with the house.

If the above sounds a little far fetched, just think of this: in

The antiques business is an interior decorating business.

Grapevine we have a developer who undertakes a promotion called "The House of Dreams" every time he opens a new subdivision. His interior decorator always called me to decorate a room in a show house to help them sell their new models. "Sure," I would say, "as long as your sales staff sell my furniture if a customer expresses interest in buying it."

Guess how many times the developer bought the antique English halltree just to close a sale?

In closing this section I would like to say that new marketing techniques are only limited by one's imagination. Customers look to you to give them ideas. If you can satisfy this by packaging, presentation, or by offering your antiques in a unique way, they will love you for it. Not only that, they will recommend you to their friends, thereby broadening your all-important customer base.

Mixing antiques with interior decorations

"The antique business is an interior decorating business," I said two years ago and the same holds true today, probably even more so. As antiques become more mainstream due to an increasingly larger segment of the buying public realizing that antiques can be used as terrific mix-'n-match pieces, so the antique business will have to cater to this trend or lose out to other furniture manufacturers.

I, therefore, recommend that antique dealers sell modern decorating pieces as well as antiques. Just make sure that the modern pieces fit in with the concept of your booth. To find the best selection of interior decorating pieces, I recommend that you go to a trade show in a major city near you. Many cities like Dallas have a World Trade Center where twice a year you can view a tremendous variety of interior decorating products. You'll be surprised to even find products that look like antiques, but are

The odd modern sofa looks good and helps sell your antiques.

I recommend that dealers sell modern decorating pieces in addition to antiques.

really not. That's because the far eastern manufacturers grasped the fact that the antiques and interior decorating businesses are inter-related. While enthusiastically endorsing modern decorating pieces as a profitable sideline, I would remind you that they are a sideline, and not your main business. I've seen too many antique businesses forget that and end up closing down, because they start to carry only new products. A small business simply

Bigger is definitely better.

cannot compete with the big stores selling the same lines. Don't even try. Think of it this way.

A customer will be happy to pay a few dollars more for a set of modern candlesticks if she is buying an antique dresser from you that she can't buy anywhere else, but she won't be so interested in shelling out money just for the candlesticks if she can get them cheaper at Pier 1. Get the picture?

Mix modern decorator items **among** your antiques and make extra add-on sales. Just don't keep stocking new items because they are easier to obtain than antiques, or you'll find yourself going out of business very quickly. You won't be able to compete with modern products without the special edge that antiques give you.

Using mainstream furnishings

Using modern furnishings in your booth is not a bad idea if you restrict them to fabrics and selected pieces. Just don't go overboard for the same reasons outlined in the paragraph above. The odd modern sofa looks good and helps sell your antique buffets, bookcases, accessory tables, and halltrees. Remember that antiques are unique pieces and you can charge unique prices for that very reason. Since they are one-off's the customer feels special and they can't go around the corner to compare prices at another retailer. It's your edge. Just don't forget it.

Consigning

Danger! danger! danger!—unless you have it very, very, tightly under control. Then it's okay as long as the consignment is for a **very specific time only.**

Consigning to a builder for a show house when using a "new marketing technique" will work well. Consigning to another dealer will not! First, the house builder will have more money and will agree to buy the item if it gets damaged in his care. Another dealer will not. They are liable to tell you that it's part and parcel of the business. Furthermore, the builder will definitely sell your huge bookcase if it helps him sell his $200,000 house.

The competitive antiques dealer will try to pursuade the customer to buy his own unit first to make more than the 10 percent sales commission you both agreed to.

Nothing more needs be said about consigning. Do it for a marketing reason only, not just to help another dealer out. Use it, but don't abuse it. It will become counterproductive if you do.

Which brings me to combining operations.

Combining operations

A great idea if done for the right reasons.

"You're crazy," I can immediately hear you say. "First you say don't consign, and now you are advocating combining operations. Surely it's the same thing, just on a larger scale?"

"No, it's not."

Consigning works to the advantage of the consignee, not the consignor. They get the piece to sell and make a profit, albeit a small one, without laying out any money. In combining operations, both parties reduce their overheads, as well as becoming one big operation instead of two small ones. That's the difference. Not only that, in combining operations both parties have an interest in selling everything, not just their own inventory. That's why I recommend it. Just like the hardware stores have found since the Home Depot and Lowes chains appeared on the scene, the bigger you are the more customers you attract. Bigger is definitely better. It works the same way in the antiques business.

Not only does being bigger draw in more customers, it also gives you more help and you can, therefore, get a break when you need one. Sound good? You bet!

One caution however. If you are going to combine operations with another antique dealer, first make sure you know them really well. Next, write everything down. How much you are both putting in, how the work is going to be shared, and how the expenses and profits will be paid and distributed are very important details to settle beforehand. Don't leave anything to chance. Write it down, both parties sign it, and then like a pre-nuptial agreement, it becomes binding.

Combining antique operations makes good business sense—just write things down like a business and not like a friendship.

 **Checklist**

- ❐ **Updating your operation.** Set up a routine, split your booth or store into sections, change out one section every two weeks, use your imagination and display that old lattice work, the wine barrel, and that distressed Dutch dog cart to the max! Your customers will love your displays and think that you have the most interesting booth in the mall, if not in the whole town. Maybe even in the whole state!

- ❐ **Learning from the past.** Feature seasonal items such as antique bibles for Christmas and watch last year's stock fly out the door. Record keeping becomes very important for this marketing aspect of your antique business, and computers become invaluable for this task. They take out the hard work, so get one.

- ❐ **Coping with changes.** Keep your ears to the ground and you'll score big. Be ahead by picking up on trends early. In that way you'll sell fast and won't have any dead inventory left over.

- ❐ **New marketing techniques.** Combine a punch bowl, a bottle of wine, antique napkins and coupons into a "Royal Collection" to maximize your sales. Watch the displays fly out the door!

- ❐ **Mixing antiques with interior decorations.** Good idea as long as you control the decorations. Don't overdo them for maximum effect. Less is best.

- ❐ **Mainstream furnishings.** Add the odd richly upholstered sofa for homeyness, but not more. Remember that you are an antique dealer not a mainstream furniture retailer.

- ❐ **Consigning.** Don't do it unless it's a specific marketing strategy and then keep track of the consigned goods like a hawk. Always set a time limit on the consigned goods.

❐ **Combining operations.** Bigger is better for business, but sign a pre-nuptial agreement detailing who does what and who gets what share. Don't forget, divorces get messy. I wholeheartedly recommend dealers to do this by combining their operations.

We've come to the end of chapter three. It's been fun and I look forward to chapter four which covers how all the new electronic technology now affects an antiques dealer.

Since this is the single biggest change affecting the antiques business in the last three years, I think it is a very important chapter. Let's go for it, shall we?

Chapter 4

Antiques in the Technology Age

Like all businesses today, the antiques business is being affected by new technology. Faxes, personal computers, the Internet and voice mail are now all essential tools of the trade in operating even a part-time antiques business, let alone a full-time one. Dealers that embrace this new technology will thrive, those that don't will have a hard time just keeping up, and may not survive. But it shouldn't be a question of survival. It should be a question of welcoming these new tools to make your antiques business more profitable, easier to operate, more efficient, and even more fun to operate than it has been in the past.

Just think of the new opportunities technology will open up. And with half the effort!

You like that, don't you? I thought you would. We all like things easier, especially if they help us make **more money from antiques**.

However, many people, including myself, are confused by all the electronic gadgetry flooding the market.

"I don't even know how to switch a computer on," some of my antique dealer friends say, and of course that's not really true. What they really mean to say, if I may be so presumptuous, is that they are so overwhelmed by all the technical jargon that gets pumped out, that their confidence in ever understanding DOS, RAM, 53Kbps, MHz and Windows 95 is at rock bottom. And I bet some of you feel like that yourself, don't you? I know I do.

The biggest thing that confuses me, is that every time I finally understand one system or piece of software, it changes. I mean, look at all the Windows **something-or-others** that are around. It seems that every year I have to start learning all over again! What a bore.

Don't worry about it. One thing that I have learned is that I'm not an expert and that you don't have to be one either. I do, however, know how to use a computer to further an antiques business, and in simple terms I will pass that on to you. There will be no heavy discussions on the relative merits of the new 56K modems that enable you to access the Internet at zap speed, or even on the dispute between Microsoft and Netscape regarding their browsers. Just practical advice on using what is available, how to find it, and how to use it in simple, logical steps. Those of you who are computer nerds can move on as the advice I will give is already well known to you. Those that are like me, however, will find what I am about to say very useful.

Electronic tools for the antiques business—which, what, and why

So what new technology should an antiques business have at its disposal?

Well how about the new Polaroid cameras? Unlike the old ones, the new models are very compact and give great picture clarity. This is a very useful tool for the antique dealer. It enables you to take an instant shot, let the customer take it home to show her husband or better half and before you know it—you've sold the huge buffet! Seeing is definitely believing. A Polaroid camera is a simple, but very effective, tool. No dealer should be without one.

The second tool that a dealer can't do without is voice mail. Everyone knows how that works so I won't cover it, save to say that you should remember what its purpose was before voice mail came with all the bells and whistles. Voice mail's purpose is to ensure that you do not miss a customer's call, period! Everything else is superfluous to that central dictate.

Pagers serve the same purpose. Use them. Don't forget that nothing is more irritating than not being able to get ahold of someone once you have decided to buy an antique. For some reason spending money builds resentment against the seller! Just look how cranky airline passengers get. You can almost see them fume: "All that money for a scrappy piece of paper!" That they are getting efficient transportation doesn't seem to register. I was going to say cheap, but the way airfares are rising I don't think I will. But to get back to the point. In order to return messages or calls, you have to get them. You can't wait a week until you visit your booth. Get a pager, advertise its number, and call the customer back post haste.

As the antiques business gets more sophisticated, faxes are also becoming an essential tool. No longer just an instrument for stockbrokers or mega deal makers, sending or receiving a fax has replaced letters where documentation is required. If you want to be sure that the buffet you are buying sight unseen is exactly as you picture it, get the seller to take a Polaroid shot and fax it to you. Auctioneer's terms of business, price confirmations, offers to buy—all should be faxed when a written record is necessary. Faxes and voice mail can now even be sent or received through your computer. This is great if you don't have that much fax usage as it saves you the extra cost of a separate machine. I would, however, recommend that you get yourself a stand alone fax machine and a dedicated phone line if you envisage expanding in the antiques business. They are well worth it, as they are relatively cheap and save your phone line from being tied up for long periods. With the price of fax/phone machines now down around $300, they are almost as cheap as a sophisticated voice mail machine alone. Which brings us to the personal computer.

Computers and antiques

Before buying a computer, consider what uses you have for it in your antiques business.

The object is to get one that fulfills your needs, has capacity and capability for your likely future expansion, and has the added advantage of home use. Here I have another recommendation to save you money.

You don't need one with all the bells and whistles.

Don't spend money on capability that you don't need and that you will never use. If you do, you will have spent money that can be put to far better use. Just remember, computers can always be upgraded as the need arises and in any case, they are outdated so fast, that two years from now you might want to change it completely. Buy one that does what you need with some reserve and not one that has bells and whistles that you won't even look at and which costs you the earth.

So what kind of computer and software do you need to run your antiques business?

You need one that can run your accounts, keep your records, allow you to access the Internet and has sufficient hard disk storage to maintain at least five years of business operations, i.e., almost any one that you can buy off the shelf today.

Of these four functions, the Internet one requires the more up-to-date capabilities.

As I mentioned at the beginning of this chapter, I don't intend to get highly technical in recommending a computer to run an antiques business. I will, however, cover three features that are important for the computer illiterate antique dealer to know when purchasing a computer.

The first is RAM (Random access memory). To my way of thinking, RAM is the **working capacity** in the computer that the antiques dealer has available when entering his records, doing his accounts, or recording antique prices. All an antiques dealer needs to know is that you want 16mb of RAM as a minimum. If you need more later on you can add extra RAM to give you up to a total of 128mb if you are into heavy graphics. Many computers now come standard with 32mb, which is more than enough for you. Ram is therefore, **memory to work with,** and the thing to remember is that you don't starve the computer; 16mb or 32mb is what you need.

$ $ $ $ $

The second feature that is important is hard drive capacity. This means computer storage capacity and is easy to recommend since most computers now come with a 1.8 to 2.1gb (gigabytes—almost sounds like an antique doesn't it?) hard drive. Now forget about this. Who cares if you have 2.1 billion units of storage? It's more than most of us will ever need. And if you need more? I doubt you ever will but if you do, just buy a bigger hard drive when, and only when, you need it!

The third computer feature that is of interest to you as an antique dealer is the modem. The modem is the electronic gizmo that allows you **to talk over the phone line**. It enables you to access the Internet and use your computer as a fax or as a voice mail gadget. You need a 33.6K data/14.4 Fax modem, and since most computers come with this now built in, all you have to remember is to check that it has one. New 56K modems are now flooding the market and prices have dropped from $700 to $200 in just a year. If you want to invest extra anywhere, this is where you should do it, but only after you have invested in 32mb of RAM first.

Now that we have covered the hardware features you need in a computer, we will discuss software. This is far more important.

As we all know (really?), all that hardware is totally useless, because to make it work we need the software programs. Any task we want to do requires them. For me to discuss this is very easy. All I can say is: "Go see your local computer store, tell them what you want to do, test the software programs that suit your requirements best, and before buying, make sure that your computer doesn't already have it loaded in-factory, which it probably does."

See, I told you that all this electronic wizardry is simple. For those that have never used a computer, the above is all that you need to know when purchasing one for your antiques business. At present prices (December 1997) such a computer should cost you from $1000 to $1500 complete with monitor. For those that are experts, don't write telling me I am an ignoramus please, write to your computer book author. This is a book about antiques, not electronics, thank you!

One final thing. Many computer manufacturers now build-to-order at the same price as you can buy a ready-made off-the-shelf unit. One hears good things about Gateway and Dell in particular. My suggestion is go that way. If you do, you will have an expert walk you through your required hardware. Just remember that you are the boss and only purchase what you absolutely need.

Taking advantage of new opportunities

Now that you have all the basic information about what features you need in a computer, let's think about the uses for this sexy looking machine that you have so lovingly brought home and for which you have mortgaged your life.

To do that, ask yourself the basic question again:

"What do you need the computer for in your antiques business?"

Record keeping, price comparisons, accounts, customer details, seasonal information, profit and loss, producing flyers—the list goes on and on. Just remember, it's a tool to help you run your business, not a replacement for good planning, common sense, or on-the-ball management. For those functions you need to use that other computer—your brain!

The Internet—Cyberspace!

That brings me to the World Wide Web. Called cyberspace, surfing the net, and all the other catch phrases that are on everyone's lips these days. The use of the Internet is now an essential tool in operating your antiques business. The reason is that it has opened a whole new market in which to buy and sell antiques, get information, appraise antiques, and locate special pieces at a cost of only $8 to $20 per month, depending on which server you prefer. That's got to be the best value for money I have ever seen.

"Server? What's a server?" I already hear you asking.

The server is the company that connects you via your phone line to this exploding information world.

For those of you antiques dealers that live on the planet Earth, let me give you an overview of how the antiques business works on the Internet. Just picture it as a book. Open the book (connect to the Internet), turn to the antique section (select a search engine and type in the word "antiques"), look up the section you want (select a Web page that claims to have what you are looking for) and bingo! All the information that you could possibly want is at your fingertips. You can sell antiques, buy antiques, get information on antiques, find addresses of dealers, look up books on antiques, etc. etc. Here I want to insert a plug. Look up my first book, *Money from Antiques*. It's there under my name and under Krause, my publisher's name.

And all this can be done on a worldwide basis in the comfort of your living room!

Incredible when you think about it, isn't it?

Just remember two things. The first is: Don't get scared of the Internet. You can't blow it up, so explore it to your heart's content. The second is: Don't let it dominate your life. It's very addictive.

Taking advantage of this new electronic opportunity

In the next chapter I will discuss buying and selling on the Internet but first let's cover a few basics.

The success of your antiques business will depend on your personality and on your efforts, not on some technology, good will, or even on anything I say. It is you, and you alone, that has to put in the effort to succeed by thinking things through first, and then using all available tools and advantages. In practice, this means that you don't give up redecorating your booth just because you sold a nice piece on the Internet, or that you don't stop writing thank-you notes to suppliers just because you bought some candles at a better price via the Web. Just remember, nothing will ever replace that personal contact when you meet customers face to face in your booth on a Saturday afternoon. That's what the antiques business is all about—personal contact and service.

Web sites

Sounds like something out of a Spider-Man cartoon, doesn't it? Just think of web sites this way. An antique web site on the Internet is simply an electronic brochure detailing a specific antique subject. And there are plenty of those, believe me. Web sites on collectibles, memorabilia, furniture, perfume bottles, antique tours, paintings etc., etc., etc. and even more etceteras. Anything that you want to know about antiques is on a web site. And I mean anything. Incredible!

Accessing these web sites is very easy. This is what you do. Get connected with your server, America Online, GTE Internet, Flashnet or any one of a dozen others. Follow the instructions and select a search engine. You will see these listed. All of them are good, although they vary in efficiency. I like to use Yahoo! for main selections and Alta Vista for more specific searches. When the box comes up just type in "antiques" or "antiques for sale." This will throw up dozens of titles such as "Commerce and business-antiques." Click on one of these and you will get a whole menu of antique products, services, and submenus. Easy isn't it? Now you can buy, sell, peruse and even giveaway antiques to your heart's delight. Just remember that you have a wife/husband/children/girlfriend/boyfriend in your life and that they will get very upset if you forget them for hours at a time. The Internet can get very addictive. As I said before, just remember that it's a tool to be used among a whole lot of tools, and that antiques should be a fun part of your life and not an all-consuming addiction. Passion, yes. Addiction, no.

$ $ $ $ $

For you who are computer experts the above is pretty basic, but just remember how confusing it all was when you were starting out. If you know of any of your antiques friends or acquaintances just signing on, please help them. Fun, a helping hand, and camaraderie—that's what the antiques business is all about.

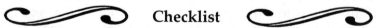 Checklist

- [ ] **Antiques in the Modern World.** Use voice mail, Polaroid cameras, pagers, faxes, and personal computers to be successful in the antiques business.
- [ ] **Computers.** Purchase one that does what you want, has some expansion capability and save your money on the

bells and whistles. They only cost hard-earned money and don't help that much.

- ❐ **Taking advantage of the new opportunities**. Use them to help you run your business more efficiently, but don't forget the basics of customer service—the right products and service with a smile.

- ❐ **Cyberspace!** Get on the Internet for great opportunities and information at a bargain price. This is definitely value for money.

- ❐ **Taking advantage of the Internet.** There are many advantages and I cover them in the next chapter. Just don't lose sight of the fact that it is a tool, and just a tool.

- ❐ **Web sites.** Sounding like something out of a Spider-Man movie, these are only electronic brochures detailing specific products or services. Click onto "Antiques" and surf to your heart's content.

I hope that you found this simple introduction to the cyberspace world interesting. It is the single most revolutionary thing to happen to the antiques industry since the advent of the antique mall. In the following chapter I will get down to the business of selling and buying antiques using this new medium. It should be fun and I look forward to having you along!

Chapter 5

Buying on the Internet is the Future

The Internet opens up a wonderful supply of products to the professional antique dealer.

Hundreds of web sites offer everything from antique thimbles to nine-foot-high antique bookcases. If you are looking for it, you'll find it on the Internet. But like most things in life, everything does not always come up smelling roses.

First let's consider how buying antiques on the Internet works.

Starting with the basics, switch on your computer, connect to your provider, and punch in a search engine of your choice. Type in the words "antique-buying." A whole bunch of submenus in categories for almost every antique product that you can think of will come up. Select the product line you want and voila! Hundreds and hundreds of suppliers of that unusual, rare, antique item that you were so desperately looking for. Descriptions, sizes, colors and markings, it's all there on the computer screen. Some suppliers even have pictures that you can download via your color printer to entice you even more.

That's where the trouble starts.

First of all you have to contact the seller on their e-mail address. That in itself is easy, but how do you know who you are dealing with and where they are? They could be in Timbuktu, for all you know, or just around the corner. Without asking there is simply no way of knowing their physical location, although now, some do add that to their product offers.

More important, how do you know that you will get the goods once your hard-earned money is in their hands? The seller will want payment up front. You don't want to part with it until you are sure that the antique is exactly as described and that you will actually get it. Therein lies the biggest problem. Unless the seller is in a city near you, this is one major headache of a difficulty.

"Ask them to send it FedEx collect," I hear someone say.

Sure. Except that FedEx, or any other parcel service, will not guarantee what is in the parcel. They will guarantee that they'll deliver it, but not the authenticity of its contents. Nor will they allow you to open the box while they wait. The risk of potential lawsuits is too great. That's where buying antiques on the World Wide Web hits a major snag—either the buyer or the seller has to trust the other person to some extent.

Unless you can come to an agreement with the seller, the only other way to buy reasonably safely on the Internet is by using a listed brokerage service. Internet web sites, such as those of a company called Treasure Chest, advertise that they will give you a money back guarantee should you not be satisfied. They also say that a credit is arranged if you are not completely satisfied with your purchase through them. The two statements differ slightly and I would make sure that you clarify this before purchasing anything. After all, if the product is not as advertised when you get it, you want your money back and not a credit to buy something else that is listed on their web page. Who wants a vase, when your customer needs a mirror, right?

$ $ $ $ $

For those buyers wanting confirmation that they will not lose their money to a scoundrel that simply takes your payment and doesn't send the product, or sends you a product substantially different from that advertised, these brokerage services might be worthwhile. But it doesn't come without cost. Most brokerage operators charge the seller a commission of around 18%, as well as a $15 charge for digitizing an image of the product, so the service is not cheap.

The problem is that these brokerage houses only have limited offerings as they face the same problem that you do, namely that a customer has to send them the antique for them to be able to guarantee its details and to digitize its image onto their web page.

While I think such brokerage services are more secure than making your own private deal, such as paying half on purchase and half on delivery and inspection, I hesitate to recommend them. One always has to remember that Internet operators are extremely difficult to locate and even if one can do so, after considerable time and effort, how do you collect your refund without considerable legal bills? Not only that, if the broker files for bankruptcy once they have collected enough money from multiple dealers, you certainly won't get anything back through the bankruptcy court.

So how do you buy on the Internet with reasonable security?

The method of payment that I recommend as being as safe as you can get, is payment via a credit card. Before you use this method however, call your credit card company and find out what their conditions for paying the supplier are. Most credit card companies operate their transaction services through bank clearing operations who take between three days and four weeks to pay the claimant. Use one that takes as long as possible. American Express is one that springs to mind. When I had my antique store, American Express took up to 30 days to pay the merchant. This time lag will enable you to receive the product, check it, and accept or return it to the seller.

I would however recommend that you discuss this thoroughly with the supplier.

$ $ $ $ $

Explain your concerns, tell them which card you are going to use, advise them of your credit card company's merchant payment conditions, and even suggest they call the company to get confirmation. Be fair. Most sellers are genuine and are not out to steal your money. They deserve being treated as fairly as you, the purchaser, does.

Discussing your payment concerns and your intention to use the card company's good offices to ensure that you are not taken also serves a second purpose—that is to gauge the seller's honesty. It stops you from wasting your time and going through the whole negotiating process for nothing.

Here, a bit of advice on psychology helps. If the seller suddenly gets aggressive or balks too strongly at working with you through your card company, you can bet that all is not well. Now I'm not talking about the usual concerns that a private seller might have such as not having accepted a credit card to sell something before. I'm talking about the seller that suddenly starts accusing you of not trusting them, or the seller that makes out that the product is absolutely as he or she says so and who are you to doubt their word? Just remember, if you have any doubts at all, pass on the purchase and keep looking. There will be many more ruby glass vases on the Internet, if not today, certainly next week. You can bet on that. That's the American system after all—where there's a willing buyer there's bound to be a willing seller!

Having said all that, I recently had a friend call me up and tell me that they bought some wonderful antiques on the Internet, paid by cheque, and had no trouble whatsoever. This shows that there are still many honest folks around. I wouldn't recommend this however. It will only take one bad apple and my friend will lose all the profit she made, and more. Err on the side of caution, that is what I would recommend. Oh, one more thing, and this is important. To make this credit card form of payment work, you will have to get the product sent overnight. That means you will have to pay the extra freight charge at the very least. You simply cannot expect the seller to bear this extra cost, but if you have discussed everything thoroughly with the antique's owner, you might find that they would consider car-

Imagine you've seen a wonderful coffee table.

rying half the difference between the ordinary and the overnight freight charge.

In addition, one very important thing you should do with all transactions is to document everything. And I mean everything. Every tiny detail. Write it all down in the form of a diary. The credit card company will hold up payment to the merchant on your say-so, but only until they hear both sides of the dispute. It is possible that after due consideration, they will still go ahead and finalize the transaction, in which case they will debit your account. By supplying full documentation such as the Internet advertisement (print it out for reference), a copy of the delivery note, the receipt for freight, Polaroid photographs of the antique delivered, and a copy of your **registered** letter rejecting the purchase, your credit card company will have a valid reason for stopping payment. Don't forget that they, like you, have to protect themselves from frivolous lawsuits. It will also help you to protect yourself, should such an eventuality ever happen to you.

$$\$ \ \$ \ \$ \ \$ \ \$$

One more thing. Should you reject the goods, please pay the return freight costs yourself. I know that many people will disagree with me on this point, claiming that the seller was misleading and should be responsible for the extra cost, but just remember that you are not in a fight, you just want to get what you ordered. Lest you think that I'm an old softy, also remember that it will give you a reason to counter sue should the antique seller be an obnoxious and aggressive bully. What small claims court judge, or any judge for that matter, can find against you if you have demonstrated goodwill towards the deceitful seller?

So is buying on the Internet effective?

Considering how it opens up a whole new source of supply, its potential is unlimited.

With cyberspace working for you, you have the whole world as your supplier and not just your local auctioneer. It puts you in a far stronger position than if you hadn't taken advantage of this new technology. And if fears of getting ripped off are too much for you to cope with, you can still buy only from sellers in your state, greater area, or even in your town. They also advertise on the Internet and you wouldn't have known about them had you not located them electronically.

One other very important use of the Internet is to help you establish price guides.

Remember there is no substitute for knowledge when buying antiques.

Imagine you've seen a wonderful Queen Anne coffee table at the auctioneer's Saturday viewing period. All excited, you rush home and check the equivalent **offers** on the Internet. With the selling price finalized in your mind, you can now either call in an absentee bid or be pretty confident of your maximum buying limit when you are at the auction the next day. By checking the equivalent **sales** prices for Queen Anne tables by retail antique stores with their own web sites, you will have almost a 100% accurate purchase and sale price, before you get involved in the hurley-burley of bidding at the auction. Just think of what a comfort that would be, especially if the price at the auction skyrockets and you lose the piece that you had set your heart on buying. You won't really care, will you? Not only can you buy another equivalent piece on the Internet, but you know that it wasn't such a good deal after all.

Protecting yourself

Even though I have already covered a number of points on how you should protect yourself from being ripped off, there is one thing more important than taking elaborate precautions.

Remember that there is no substitute for knowledge when buying antiques. This holds true whether you are buying at auction, privately, from another dealer, or on the Internet. If you know everything about Majolica—what that means, that Majolica products were made in different countries, colors that were used, styles, type of products made, etc.—then no one can pull the wool over your eyes. As I said before in *Money from Antiques*, if you know your business you are an expert, and being an expert means constantly updating your knowledge.

Where do you get all this vast knowledge from? On the Internet of course! You knew that? Hot dog! I knew you were smart. But not just on the Internet right? At your local library, at your local bookshop, at antique seminars and by listening to

The more knowledge you have, the less risk there is of buying a dud.

dealers specializing in certain antique products—the more knowledge you have, the less risk there is of buying a dud. Just don't blame yourself too much if you slip up. We all do, even me. The light oak bookcase that I once thought was made in France in 1890 still comes back to haunt me every now and then. What a boo-boo. How the manufacturer managed to produce such a great reproduction I do not know! Just try not to let it happen to you.

Surfing the net for antique products

Surfing. Sounds fun, doesn't it? Almost like going to Hawaii, or Huv-I-eeee, as they say. Surfing the Internet for products can take time. You'd be surprised how much! Just don't break up your marriage over it. Or let your business fall apart. Like everything, plan which sites you are going to check out on a regular basis, do that in the minimum time, spend a few minutes checking some others, and then move on. That's how to use the net.

Surf by all means, but only after your work is done. As an afterthought: If you really want to surf, why don't you surf by looking up the football scores. The relaxation will do you good. After that, turn to your accounts and deal with **them**! They are on the same computer remember?

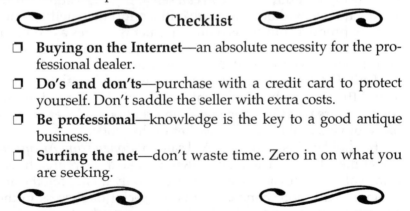

Checklist

☐ **Buying on the Internet**—an absolute necessity for the professional dealer.

☐ **Do's and don'ts**—purchase with a credit card to protect yourself. Don't saddle the seller with extra costs.

☐ **Be professional**—knowledge is the key to a good antique business.

☐ **Surfing the net**—don't waste time. Zero in on what you are seeking.

We have come to the end of buying on the Internet. It's vital for all antique dealers.

With this chapter, and the following chapter on 'Selling on the Internet' under your belt, it will be easy—and eventually fun. That's what it's all about, isn't it? Making money while having fun, right? It will be.

Chapter 6

*M*oney, Money, Money, from Cyberspace?

Selling on the Internet

What an exciting prospect selling on the Internet is! Just imagine this. Your customer base is no longer restricted by the number of people visiting your booth in a mall, or your Main Street store. Selling your antiques is no longer bound by regular business hours, by the number of hours you work yourself, or even by night or day. Now you can sell antiques 24 hours a day, 7 days a week, without any more initial effort than getting your antique products out on as many Internet web sites as you can. Furthermore, your market is now no longer just your local area, your town or even your state. It is now the whole world.

Isn't that an exciting prospect? I love it. And so should you. Your little antique business, which was only known in the surrounding area, has just become an international player accessible to buyers in the furthest reaches of the globe.

But hold on just a minute. As I said in *Money from Antiques*, sometimes it's better to slow down, to take a deep breath, become coldly professional, and then, and only then, grab the advantages with both hands. That is the secret of success in the antique business, and in any business come to think of it.

How do you do that?

By formulating a plan before you take this exciting and potentially highly productive leap into cyberspace marketing, that's how! And once you do that, write it down as a guide for when the deluge of inquiries start to pour in for your products.

Okay, enough of the hard sell. Let's get on with the nuts and bolts of selling on this wonderful new antique medium.

Like buying on the Internet, selling on the Internet is a relatively simple thing to set up.

Dozens and dozens of web sites exist for advertising your product. And it's simple to list them. All you have to do is follow the same procedure I outlined in buying on the Internet by logging on, selecting a search engine, typing in 'antiques-selling' this time, and voila! Now all you have to do is fill in the form that pops up on your screen and the world is your oyster.

So why did I say slow down earlier on?

Because, like everything else in life, all is not as simple as it seems. Problems exist, but so do advantages. "It's like food," someone once told me. "It needs a lot of preparation to make it taste good." And the same goes for selling on the Internet. By the way, if I offend anyone with my comments, please forgive me. I am so enthusiastic about every experience in life, whether it's good, bad, and even downright ugly, that I sometimes get carried away. I sometimes think that life is like antiques. They satisfy all tastes. More important to antique dealers, someone wants them badly enough to buy them!

Enough of the frivolity. Let's start with the advantages of Internet trading, shall we?

Advantages of selling on the Internet

First of all, I want you to remember the problem we had with buying on the Internet, the one about not wanting to get ripped off. Well, now the shoe is on the other foot and you are the one who has to get organized so that your customer feels comfortable in dealing with you. Not just comfortable, but trusting. Well, we know how to tackle the payment problem now don't we?

Since you already have a booth or antique store, you already have the setup for dealing with credit cards, don't you? See how easy it is? Yes, that's right. No credit, no layaway, no deposit, and no hold-it-to-the-end-of-the-month. Suggest that your Internet customer pay for the product that you are advertising with their credit card. Not only that, give them the same courtesy that you expected when buying on the Internet yourself, and suggest that you will hold up processing the transaction until they receive the goods, check them, and confirm that they arrived in good order. Not only that, being the good businessperson that you are, you will also agree to pay for half the extra freight to send that vase to them via the carrier's overnight service. See where I'm going with this? That's right! I'm building goodwill. And please believe me, it will stand you in good stead. After all, that customer has friends, he or she will talk, his or her friends will buy, and you won't have to go through all this rigamarole again, will you? Just like you did with your initial booth customers, and all of the ones that have visited your booth since, build goodwill by giving great service.

But there are also other things to remember when selling on the Internet.

First, give yourself the best chance to sell what you are advertising. Make sure that the description is full and comprehensive, that it covers all the features of the product—color, size, weight, special markings or characteristics etc., etc., etc. Get the picture now?

And how do you do this efficiently and professionally? Well you don't want to turn a customer off by rambling on and on, do you? Just remember that the average person's attention span is about 20 seconds.

$ $ $ $ $

Even in the antique business?

Sure, even more so in the antique business.

My suggestion, therefore, is this: Write the details of your product down on one of those 3 by 5 cards. Write it once, edit it, edit it, and edit it again. Conscientiously think of how you can describe it with more punch, without deleting necessary details. It's like writing—polishing your work till it sparkles is what writers call it.

Then, having gotten the description as detailed and interesting as possible, transfer it to the Internet. Taking care to describe your antique clearly and concisely will pay huge dividends, believe me. Too often I see products advertised on some web site in such a boring way that it makes me yawn before I am halfway through reading the description.

And one other thing, don't embellish. Let the detailed, pointed description speak for itself. Words such as gorgeous, wonderful and fantastic don't cut it. Better use words like clear, clarity, undamaged, no repairs. It will save you arguing with a dissatisfied customer and having to pay the return freight if you did not mention that the fruit bowl had been chipped and that the chip was repaired by an amateur.

An even more important detail to enclose is your full contact address. Don't use abbreviations. The Finnish gentleman in Helsinki won't know what WI or OH will mean.

Write Wisconsin or Ohio out in full. And don't forget to put USA or United States of America at the back of your address. We Americans might know where Kansas City is but the average Frenchman might not. Talking about that. I recently had a new rubber address stamp made. One of those that you stamp down—guaranteed for a thousand uses, they say.

Since I frequently send mail overseas, I had USA added to the mailing address. Would you believe that the manufacturer held up making the stamp for a week because he didn't know what that meant? That's the truth, believe me!

Having bombarded you with the above details, there is one more thing I suggest you put in your Internet advertisement. However, enclosing it with full product details is a double-edged sword.

I suggest that you put in your antique booth's physical address together with your mailing address. Do not enclose your home address under any circumstances, just your booth details, please. By enclosing your booth details you will make the Internet customer feel more comfortable. Just remember to tell your mall owner what you are doing so that if they get a call checking up on you, they'll know what it's all about. They should already be set up to receive your mail anyway, but it's just common courtesy to inform them that you expect this to increase considerably. You never know, other booth holders might hear about your Internet operation and ask you to help them out. You might even charge them for your services when they ask you to advertise their products on various web sites, since they don't have access to the Internet themselves.

So much for the advantages of selling on the Internet. How about the disadvantages?

Disadvantages of the Internet

There are a few disadvantages to selling on the Internet, but not many. Those that do exist are annoying. The first one is the scams that follow your first advertisement being placed. Expect a deluge of them. It seems that new Internet addresses attract a swarm of scam artists just waiting to pounce like bees to honey.

One of the regrettable factors in selling on the Internet is that your Internet address is available to every crook trying to make

a fast buck. Expect to receive solicitations from long distance telephone companies, from "incredible money making opportunity"
promoters, and even from "start your own antique business"
specialists. All of them will offer to help you make a fortune for
only $99! All you have to do, according to them, is to send this
$99 to a postal address. In cash, of course!

Whenever I get one of these solicitation messages, I type
"pull the other leg" across their wording and send it back. If I
feel really mean I tell them to go buy my books for "only
$12.95." That usually shuts them up. So, as a warning, just be
careful, expect this deluge and simply delete their e-mail without even reading the full spiel. Just be careful and make sure it's
not some customer-waxing lyrical about your own wonderful,
antique product. You'd hate yourself if you lost a sale.

The only other disadvantage of selling on the Internet that I
can think of is the proliferation of web sites. Which one should
you choose to advertise your product on?

There are so many of them.

The answer to that is, "I don't know." They are all both effective and ineffective. My suggestion is that you put your offer on
as many as you can, and that in turn means that you might have
to spend a whole weekend doing it. It's well worth it, believe me.
You need to cast your net as wide as possible to succeed.

Which brings us to the next section.

How effective is selling on the Internet?

I wish I could say 100 percent effective, but like all things in
life, nothing is guaranteed.

This lack of certainty can be for a variety of reasons, not just
the obvious ones of price, product quality, or lack of demand.

Having studied sales on the Internet, I don't really know why
products sometimes elicit incredible responses from antique Internet surfers, and sometimes it's as if the advertisement never exist-
ed. I guess it's just supply and demand in the end. One thing to
remember is this: even when you think the whole world has turned
off their computers, you can still help sell your product quicker.
And how do you do that? Just do your homework, that's how.

Check for the best web pages to advertise that silver antique
tea set—the site that is full of them is obviously your first
choice. Customers will browse the one that specializes in tea
sets first. Pretty obvious, isn't it? And if you are selling an antique train set, peruse the sites that specialize in railway related

He doesn't need to respect that picture that you are selling in a quiet place.

products and memorabilia first. Even more important, double check the advertisements on those web sites every week to see which offers are no longer there. It gives you an indication that "Joe Bloggs Antique" page is active. Most important of all, check out the web site's "hit" figures. For those just starting out, "hit" means someone logging on to the site. The more "hits"— the more potential buyers. Obvious isn't it?

How do you find out the "hit" figures? Well, most web sites list them in their address details. If they don't, send an e-mail to the address shown and ask for the "hit" total.

Here I would reiterate what I have said before. To ensure that you are giving yourself the best chance to sell your product, make sure that your entry has full details and specifications with as much brevity and clarity as possible. Also ensure that your address is clearly visible, particularly your Internet e-mail address.

Protecting yourself

I have already covered some of the do's and don'ts in protecting yourself when selling on the Internet in the above sections, but I want to cover one aspect of human behavior that is more prevalent when selling antiques on the Internet than it is when you are dealing with customers in your booth. Just remember that we all tend to be more open when we are not face to face with the person we are talking to. It makes it easier for us to open up.

Be careful and remember what you are using the antique web site for. You are selling antiques professionally, not spouting forth in some public forum where you have a built-in resistance to persistent questioning.

My advice is this, please be careful. Just because someone expresses interest in buying the buffet that you have been trying to sell for months and you need the money desperately, don't let it slip that your mall owner opens up for business every morning at nine when there's no help around. And don't, under any circumstances, agree to meet the supposed buyer anywhere other than at your booth or in a restaurant where there are other patrons about. He doesn't need to inspect that picture that you are trying to sell in a quiet place. In public will do. Remember, this is a cruel world and antiques draw a criminal element that thinks everyone in the antique business is mega rich. As for the antique auctioneer that tells you that he saw your entry on the Internet and can sell your piece at twice the price in his auction, tell him to send his auction details to your mall address, visit his auctions at least five times, ask around about his reputation, and then, and only then, agree to meet with him.

$ $ $ $ $

Talking about letting your guard down on the Internet reminds me of a friend of mine.

Checking her e-mail one day, she was surprised to get a message from a total stranger. Apparently, she had misdirected one of her messages and it had gone to him by mistake. Flattered at his reply she sent back an apology. Within a week he was chatting with her like he was an old friend. When she told me about this I was curious and asked her if I could read his messages without prying. She agreed and I was horrified to see that he was using a classic interrogation technique. In between his innocent questions and flattery, he had obtained her street address, the fact that she was single and attractive, that she had received a divorce settlement, and that she closed up her decorating business by herself late at night, after all her staff had left. Don't do it! Cut strangers that contact you on the Internet off immediately.

Enough of the gloom and doom. Selling antiques on the Internet is terrific. Use it and be specific while keeping your guard up. Take advantage of it properly and it will work for you. You cannot afford not to.

Spreading your risk

The risks in selling on the Internet are three-fold.

First there is the risk of you releasing too much information about yourself. I have covered that already. "Just keep your guard up" is the best advice I can give you. Keep tight-lipped until you get comfortably certain that the person on the other end is a genuine customer and not some rip-off artist.

The second risk to guard against when selling on the Internet is the one about losing your money, i.e., sending the product without guaranteed payment. Since we have that one covered by insisting on payment via a credit card, that should just about take care of itself.

Stick to it. Don't let a sob story sway you. Under no circumstances send the goods before payment is in the bank, or at least in the credit card company's bank!

The third risk is the one of breakage. And this is far more important than you think, unless you are one of those professionals that I keep talking about and have already called up UPS, FedEx, the Post Office, or even your interstate transporter and checked on their insurance coverage. That's you? Great! I knew you were smart. For those that haven't, here's some advice.

$ $ $ $

Breakage or damage means loss of money—to you! Just remember that even though the customer is paying by credit card, if the goods are broken, he or she has the right to ask the card company to stop payment. One other thing, not only will damage cost you the value of the product, but it will also cost you the outbound and inbound freight when the customer rejects the goods.

So how do you avoid all the hassle of breakages? Just ask your parcel service company to mail you their packaging requirements. In addition to that, take advantage of their insurance policies to cover the cost of the product and transportation. To give you an example of how important this point is, I will relate one of my own experiences. It cost me a tremendous amount of money so I'll always remember it. In fact, it still wakes me up at night sometimes.

Back in 1992, I was shipping children's toy pianos all over the United States through my import/export company. At that time I thought I knew how to package them properly. They had come all the way from Brazil after all! Even though they were in stout boxes, I re-packed them into new cartons with two inches of polystyrene popcorn all around. Image my dismay when half the first shipment of 400 pianos came back broken. Quickly I shot around to UPS. I was full of righteous indignation and not a little worse for wear in my cheque book. Seeing how agitated I was, the UPS supervisor took me back into the warehouse and showed me what happens to the parcels when they come down a sorting chute. It was almost as if the parcel was dropping from 20 feet. Watching the boxes hit the stop bar at the bottom I cringed from the crack of the blow. That's when I learned that UPS has specific recommendations for packing anything that you ship with them.

Do it. Follow their recommendations and you won't be stuck with a loss like I was. Not only that, use the double walled cardboard boxes and not the single walled ones. They are at least three times stronger. The addition of big and small bubble wrap will also help. As will the layer of polystyrene peanuts in between. Remember, all this is to absorb the shock, so keep it ever so slightly loose, not solid like a week-old loaf of bread. Having taken all this care, even a tank won't damage that rare Messien table lamp that you sold for a fortune to that Internet customer in Alaska, will it now?

So what does all this mean in practical terms when selling on the Internet?

It means that before you advertise your product, do your homework. Calculate the freight cost to the furthest point in the U.S. Add the cost of all the extra packing you will need to ship via parcel service. Give yourself a 10 percent extra margin for packing tape, labels, string, etc. You'll be surprised how all that adds up. On my pianos, it was $60 on a $250 item. Protect yourself and be a professional by ruthlessly calculating your packaging costs accurately. That way you will make the profit that you must to survive in the antiques business, or in any business for that matter.

Casting the widest net possible

When selling on the Internet don't be shy about advertising on every web page possible.

Use them like you would flyers. No one will complain, believe me. To do that however, you will have to allocate time for the entries. Rather than doing it all at once, getting bug-eyed from watching the computer screen too much, and then shouting at your husband/wife, spread this task out over a week. The electronic forms for advertising on the Internet are very comprehensive. Solicitation companies are now using this information to push their own products so they are very thorough. By doing a few entries each night, you'll stick with it and get good coverage. Since many web sites automatically remove the entry after every 30 to 60 days, you won't have to worry about canceling the advertisement if you have sold the product. Not unless your full e-mail box gets to you. It gets a little monotonous to hear "you've got mail" every evening if you know that you sold that antique rocking horse last month! That's unless you're lonely and have a fetish for that sort of thing, in which case, you are not operating your antique business as hard as you should be.

So! We've come to the end of selling on the Internet. Here is a review of what we covered. It will enable you to turn to the main details in this chapter quickly.

 **Checklist**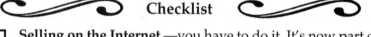

- ❑ **Selling on the Internet** —you have to do it. It's now part of every successful antique business.
- ❑ **Advantages of selling in cyberspace**—by accepting credit cards only, you get paid right away, even as you sell 24 hours a day.
- ❑ **The disadvantages of selling in cyberspace**—you will get inundated with promotions. Ignore them totally.
- ❑ **How effective is the Internet?** —very. Check the "hits" on the selected web sites to get your product out before the largest groups of buyers.
- ❑ **Protecting yourself**—be careful what you say on the Internet. Don't give away your personal details under any cost.
- ❑ **Spread your risk**—keep your guard up and calculate your packaging costs accurately. It will ensure that you make a profit and not a loss.
- ❑ **Casting the widest net on the "Net"**—do your entries methodically and keep your life partner happy.

Chapter 7

Accounts — Essential but not much Fun

As in all businesses, keeping your accounts accurate and up to date is essential for the financial health of your antique business. Too many start-up dealers spend a lot of time and effort, not to mention tons of money, only to flounder one year later. That's because they simply did not take care of business in their enthusiasm. They say, "I marked it up double what I paid for it. How come I didn't make a profit?"

Inventory records, sales and cash flow management, purchasing totals, overhead costs and accurate projections are even more essential in the antique business with the advent of the Internet. It will be very easy to forget that you debited your business card with that $800 purchase by thinking that you will record it when the product arrives. This is simply not good enough. Don't forget that you are going to advertise it on your web site immediately, and selling it before you have the accurate amounts for the freight, insurance, and clearance, will only cause you to underprice the item. There is simply no excuse for sloppiness, no matter how tedious the book work is.

In *Money from Antiques*, I detailed the various types of record keeping that you will have to maintain as a new antique dealer and I don't intend to go over these again except as an overview. Inventory, sales, costing formulas, assets, overhead costs, and profit and loss totals should all be available on a monthly basis for the beginner, and on a weekly basis for the professional antique dealer. Fortunately, all these can now be done on a computer.

Computers make light work of running your business accounts. Tons and tons of software is available from your local computer store or even on the Internet. Programs such as Quicken, Peachtree, and Basic 5 do it all for you as long as the data is entered accurately. And that's where the trouble starts. Most of us don't want to do the boring things in life, and entering figures is certainly more boring then buying, selling, or chatting about the antiques that are such a pleasure to deal with.

Since all the accounting software programs vary in how they work, I will not spend time discussing them. I would however recommend you purchase one that you can understand and use practically. You don't need all the bells and whistles— the various permutations of the same information. You need bottom lines on the various sections of your business. Follow the instructions as detailed in the software program itself or purchase literature explaining how they work. However, I do want to put forward the following suggestions.

Before purchasing the software that seems to suit your requirement, ask the salesman to demonstrate what its main features are. Many computer stores will do this for you, no problem.

Secondly I would suggest that you ask your accountants what they recommend. If you don't use an accountant yet, just call a few on the phone, explain that you might use their services once your business is up and running and seek their brief advice. Just remember, basic is what you need. Most, I have found, use Peachtree.

Here are the account categories that an antique business needs to keep a record of.

Asset management

This is easy. Asset management is not your inventory, it's your fixed assets such as your computer, fax machine, the van you use for your business, the hand-held paint spray machine etc.

Inventory journal

The inventory journal details all saleable antiques in your business. Most electronic inventory journals have entry columns for the purchase price, taxes paid, transport costs, labor, and ancillary costs such as preparation or cleaning. A summary column tells you final on-site cost. At the bottom or on the side of these journals you have subtotals and section totals. They are useful in analyzing what expense is going up or down.

Purchases journal

This details all your purchases. This is saleable product only. It does not include cleaning materials, glues, nails, or other items required in preparing the product for sale. Those are detailed in an "overhead" or "running expenses" journal. In the purchase journal all costs pertaining to purchasing the product only are detailed. These will include taxes, transport, and delivery, and will be shown individually before being summarized in the total product cost.

A Fixed Overhead or Expense Journal

This journal details all your daily, weekly, monthly and yearly expenses. Other than your rent and possibly your utility bills, all other costs vary. It is amazing how many dealers ignore what cleaning materials, repairs and display items cost. "Oh, that's covered in the ten percent I add to my final tally," they say, not really knowing if that ten percent is enough. My advice is "be professional." You are in everything else you do, so do it in this.

Layaway Journal

Most antique dealers have a "layaway" program. Keeping track of deposits and installments avoids arguments with customers as to the conditions and amounts due of the layaway and how much has been paid. I would recommend that you print out a statement every time you get another installment paid and give it to the customer. That way they will be aware of what they have paid and what is still owing.

Believe me, most customers appreciate this. It will also avoid your being embarrassed when the customer says: "But I could swear that I paid you an installment in . . . " **Tax journal** I personally like to keep a separate tax journal for reasons of documentation. Since many malls do the sales tax for you, you do not have a permanent record for your own purposes that you can get at immediately. This journal will do that for you. It could be vital if you ever get into a tussle with the sales tax authorities or with the IRS. That's the last thing you want to do, as many dealers will tell you.

Income statement

Unquestionably the most important record you need. It tells you the overall state of your business. Many lenders require a regular income statement to support their loans—often monthly.

With the new software on the market, this can be punched up with a few key strokes, as can all these journals. No problem!

And therein lies the rub. All this technology is wonderful, as long as the data is entered on a timely and accurate basis. The question is: How do you fit this in with all the other things you have to do? My advice is: **Farm it out.** Let someone else do the nuts and bolts. I could have said 'dirty' work but I didn't. Accounts are too important an aspect of your business to denigrate them.

So what should you do to help yourself? Find a friend or acquaintance that needs extra money, that's what. This must also be someone you trust. And I mean trust! Stick all the receipts, copy cash sales, credit card slips, or bills, into separate and clearly marked envelopes. Give them to your data entry person weekly and let them enter them for you. If this is still too much for you to cope with, you could buy one of those new desk top scanners such as the excellent "Visioneer" which is only 11 inches by 2.5 inches in size.

Then you can scan, store, copy, fax, e-mail, or annotate your paperwork as you empty your organizer every day and transmit them to your part time bookkeeper on a daily basis.

The most important aspect of all this advice is that being conscientious in your record keeping keeps you on top of your business. Get behind just a bit and it takes hard work to catch up, as many dealers will agree.

$$\$ \ \$ \ \$ \ \$ \ \$$

As you can see from the brevity of this section, I do not like paperwork. I'm sure most of you don't either. Now, with modern software programs, many of which come in the initial package with your computer, you and I don't have to. All we have to do is make sure that the vital data is entered. The computer has taken the chore out of bookkeeping and now there is absolutely no excuse for not having your financial status at your fingertips on a weekly basis, if not daily basis.

Oh, and one more thing. Back up all your accounts with a hard copy every time you make an alteration or addition. One large thunderstorm, such as those that we have here in Texas, and your life will become hell. Especially if the sales tax people are chasing you about last January's figures. Having backed them up, file them please! Throwing them into that pile of paperwork won't do, will it?

 **Checklist**

❑ **Accounts are essential**—get yourself a good software program to take care of all the details. At the stroke of a key, they do all the totals and summaries for you.

❑ **Categories required**—make sure that your software has an asset management category, an inventory journal, a purchases journal, an overhead and expenses journal, a layaway journal, a tax journal, and most important, an income statement.

Now all you have to do make sure that the data entries are kept up-to-date and you are in business, are you not?

This chapter has been very brief due to the new software programs taking the chore out of account keeping. The days of hand written and mentally tallied ledgers are gone and none of us will miss them, I am sure.

While thinking about this, I whispered "Thank goodness," to myself. How I hated adding up all those figures with a calculator. I'm sure you did too! If anyone can tell me why they always came out differently, please do so!

Let's move on to chapter eight which is more exciting than the boring, but necessary, figures. As in all businesses, keeping your accounts accurate and current is essential.

Chapter 8

$\mathcal{E}$xpanding Via the Internet

Expanding your antique business

Expanding one's antique business is the dream of most dealers. And why not? Now that you are established, you're in a good location, and your sales are climbing, your thoughts naturally turn to expansion. Bigger is better! Everyone wants even more money, don't they? That's what capitalism is all about.

So how do you expand your antique business?

Cautiously, that's how.

The best way of building up your antique business is the traditional way. Now that you are established in your mall, it is better to rent another booth. After all, you've got all that inventory sitting back in your garage waiting for next month when you were going to change-out everything. The question is, is it better to use the garage for housing your car now that winter is upon you and pay the extra rent for another booth, or is it better to wait? And if your answer is "Yes.", it's better to house my car and pay the rent for another booth, then it is probably also better to get that booth in another mall and not in the same one that you're already in. Spreading out to two locations is good for business.

Having decided that two booths are better than one, you should follow the same meticulous plan that you did when you opened your current booth. Remember it? Yes, of course you do! To jog your memory I'll just go over a few points. First, follow the checklist I detailed in "Getting started" in chapter two of *Money from Antiques*. Next, allocate funds to cover start-up expenses for your new booth, This amount will be considerably less than when you first started as you already have the inventory to stock the new location. Don't forget that it will take at least two months for your sales to get into full stride. Be honest with yourself and err on the cautious side. Everything costs more than you estimate, so a ten percent safety would not be too far out. Since most of the details on expanding into a second location are already covered in *Money from Antiques* I won't go over them again. Just remember to take into consideration how close the new location is to your current one, what kind of income residents of the new area have—high, low or middle class—and what product lines you should carry in the new mall. Starting an antique lamp booth, because there isn't one in the new mall, is a better bet then carrying inventory that everyone else in the same location has.

The second method of expansion is via the Internet, now that you are such an expert at using it. Since you already have products advertised on various web pages, is it not time to have a web site of your own?

"Yes!" I hear you shout immediately, thinking of how much fun this will be.

Hold on! And the reason I say "hold on" is because like everything else in life, it will take work, work and even more work. Not only will it take considerable work to set the site up, but it will also take work to maintain it. One more factor. The technical expertise required for setting up a web page will cost you a bundle unless you are a software wizard yourself. If you

Whether you are selling via the Internet or through your new mall booth, you will still need product.

figure on $10,000 as a conservative cost to get an expert company to set up a simple web site you will understand what I mean. If you do have a bent for that sort of thing, however, I would recommend you contact a company which has an excellent web site building program. Even amateurs working carefully can build their own site with this program. The cost of this software is between $2,000 to $4,000.

One other thing for novices to remember. A web site is only the beginning, a platform so to speak. Web sites require updating at least once a week and possibly even twice. This will take at minimum of two hours three a week. Are you up to that in addition to all the other hours you spend on checking the other sites? Don't forget what I said about spreading your net. You don't want to stop everything just to concentrate on your own site now, do you?

For many antique dealers, however, expanding via the Internet is the way to go. For those that are computer literate, or want to be, expanding your antique business by having your own web site is definitely the future. It is also an opportunity to expand for those dealers that find the physical aspects of maintaining a single booth almost too much for them.

Here we need to cover a very important aspect of having your own web site. In all the excitement, I bet that you forgot that you will still have to carry inventory. Whether you are selling via the Internet or through your new mall booth, you will still have to have product. Where to store it, how much, and what kind will still tax you physically. Not only that, with more inventory you will have to set up a small warehouse type of operation and you will have to carry shelving, labeling, and packaging. In addition, your inventory control on your computer software will have to be more professional. No point in advertising a cut glass decanter on your web site, selling it, and then not being able to find it among the twenty others you also carry somewhere in that box that you put somewhere!

Technical feasibility of setting up a web site

For ninety percent of us this is not possible. Although one can now buy software to build a web site, most of us are not software literate enough to cope with it. But just because the technicalities of the actual building are too complex for us to grasp without wasting days and even weeks to get it right doesn't mean that we don't know what it's all about, does it?

When using a web site, clear and focused viewing images come into play

It's just that we are in the antique business, not in the web site building business. Mind you I said "building" not "maintaining." Even if you get someone else to build the site for you, I would suggest that you learn how to maintain it so that it doesn't continually cost you money to upgrade.

So where do you find web site builders?

"On the Internet?"

Good for you! On the Internet of course—hundreds of them. Okay not hundreds—but certainly nearly hundreds. Just remember what procedure you follow when buying insurance. Buying a web site is the same—shop around. Get the best value for your money, ask for references, check the web sites the company says it set up, and even call the owners of those sites to get confirmation that a good job was done.

So, now that you know where to get a terrific web site built for your terrific new antique expansion, I am going to give you tips on what to tell the builder you want on your site. That way you will sound like an expert just too busy selling antiques to do it yourself. Just don't tell the builder that, as he will definitely put his price up. Tell him that you need a web site because business stinks. Then haggle to get the best deal.

Here's what to tell your site builder you want featured on your Internet web page (Sounds great, doesn't it?).

Before doing that, ask yourself two questions. They are very simple, but it's surprising how many people lose track of what they want a web site for, if they don't stop to think the thing through.

The questions are: 1. What is a web site? and 2. What are the goals of your site?

1. A web site is a unique electronic brochure consisting of a blend of publishing, user interface design, and electronic technology. To use a web site, three activities come into play—reading text, viewing images, and interaction between the owner and the viewer. Bearing that in mind, you need a web site that is **easy to read, easy to view, and easy to use**. Simple, isn't it?

2. What are the goals of your site? To sell? Yes of course! But also to **attract new customers** and to **supply product information.** It's obvious that without **attracting** the customers and **supplying** them information clearly and concisely, you won't sell a thing.

So what should your web site contain?

This is what you should tell your site builder you want on your web page. In this process just remember one thing. Take charge. You may not know how to build the site, but you sure as heck know what you want on it! Or you should, since you are the antiques expert. You're paying a lot of money for someone to build this site for you, so you want it right the first time.

1. Since yours is a commercial site, customers will want to know what antiques you are selling, specific descriptions, prices, your terms of payment, where and how to pay, delivery options within the U.S. and overseas, and how a customer can contact you for further details or clarification.

2. Make sure your site is easy to use. To do this you need a simple "road map" on your web page and have new products highlighted with an electronic 'flag.' Just check out the news reports on the Internet and you will see that they use **'new'** flags for the latest updates. You should too.

3. Your web site should generate repeat visits. To do that, it needs to be clearly readable, it needs to be easily changed as you will be constantly updating it, and the graphics have to be authoritative. You are an **expert** dealer remember. No fancy little quirky figures will do. You want crests, coats of arms, and clear bold wording to stamp your antique authority on the site.

4. It must be simple. That means not too many messy graphics. These detract from the antiques you are selling. After all, most of us prefer to see cartoons than the serious stuff, but this is not a cartoon site, it's an antique selling site. Don't have anything that distracts the visitor from the full impact of your antique pieces.

5. Instruct your builder to use color wisely. Color should be used for effect only, not to distract. It should be used to draw attention to the antiques you are selling, not to entertain. Just remember that most of us only have a short 20-second attention span. Your site should focus in on the products you are selling, not on some background vineyard scene in the Sonoma valley, however nice that may look.

6. You need a **KILLER** title on your web page. Make it interesting. No "James Simon Antiques." How about "Cyberspace Antiques—Guaranteed quality and delivery at warp speed"? The subtitle must also tell the customers who you are, what you do, how good your products are and that you are solid and reliable. Example: "**Cyberspace Antiques**" is a long established *specialist* antiques dealer with **multiple** locations." Okay, so you've got one booth and one web site only and your antiques are not all good. You're still trying to off-load some of your previous inventory, the stuff you bought before you turned to purchasing quality products. But that silver teapot is very special isn't it? As are those new tapestry pictures. So you're not lying. Multiple means more than one, doesn't it? Remember, be honest where it counts but don't be shy about the really good stuff you have.

7. Keep your web site small. Remember that if it takes a "surfer" too long to download your page because you've got all sorts of junk on your site, they'll click onto the next one. Fifteen seconds is the maximum time a web site should take to download with slower modems.

8. Tell the builder to keep the images clear. Too many web site specialists use complex backgrounds to show off their computer prowess. All this does is confuse your customer who has glasses an inch thick! Remember—simple is good.

9. "No animation, please, Mr. Builder!" All this does is distract, and you don't care about the builder's skills or even paying all that extra. No thanks! No animation—leave that to Disney.

10. The **text** is crucial. It must be bold, succinct, made up of short punchy sentences, and sparkle, sparkle, sparkle. Time spent on clear text will reap dividends in sales, profits, and even more money in your pocket.

11. Frames—don't use them. They take up space, reduce the area for brief, detailed descriptions, and only increase download time. Let the product stand alone. It's far more effective that way. "Clear to see" should be your motto here.

12. Hard copy. Hard copy? Yes, what does your web site look like when it's printed out. It may look great on the screen, but when printed out all that fancy work looks cheap and nasty. Don't forget that you should be able to print it out in color and make repeats as flyers. Check what your web site looks like as hard copy to make sure that it's dignified, catchy, informative, and clear to read.

13. Advertising. What an opportunity this is! Nowadays companies put their advertising on other people's web sites. This means that you can earn money while selling your product. But only if your site is classy and angled at people with disposable incomes.

Antiques have that connotation

Sell advertising space on your web site to your local bank, mortgage company or plastic surgeon. You'll make oodles of money and it'll make your site look very, very, professional. It'll certainly give you stature! Visitors will think your business obviously carries some clout. Otherwise, why would the "First Bank of Timbuktu" advertise on **your** site? What a deal!

14. Tell your builder to place a discreet "Web Award" on your site. A nice crown will do. Everyone is doing it and 90 percent of the web sites with awards on them are in the top 5 most popularly visited sites. So it's just a bit of dressing up. Everyone's doing it. A quote from an authoritative source is even better. Just make sure that it can be verified.

15. Maintenance. Last but not least, tell your builder to make your page easy to update.

It's you that will be doing it and you will thank me profusely for this advice, believe me. Especially when that favorite game is due to start in 15 minutes and your web site needs urgent updating as you have sold three of the items on it and want to advertise some new ones.

Servicing the U.S. market via the Internet

Other than keeping up with it, this is fairly simple. The first thing you have to remember is that your market is no longer just a local one, but one covering the whole of the United States. That means that having sold your product you have to deliver it to the customer. Since we've covered all the aspects of obtaining shipping information from the parcel service providers, this is just a jog to remind you how important packaging now becomes. Using those cast-off boxes from your local supermarket to send an expensive antique product 3,000 miles across the country is no longer good enough. Now you have to pack it in double walled boxes of different sizes, use bubble wrap of at least two sizes, waterproof it in shrink wrap, and protect it with polystyrene peanuts and a whole host of caution labels, delivery notes, and record keeping. Just remember, you need to have this material handy to get the sale out quickly. The sooner the better, don't you think?

So what do you have to do to organize yourself? First make a list, then use your yellow pages to find a wholesale packaging supplier, arrange delivery, and having set up your garage or that large shed at the back as your operational headquarters, you are in business.

So what happens if you sell that terrific music box to that dear old lady in Auckland, New Zealand?

Oh, and don't forget to get a dedicated second phone line, check around to get the best business phone rates, possibly get a second sales tax number, and find out the tax regulations covering sales to areas outside your state, how to pay this, and what your collection responsibilities are! It's almost like going into business all over again, isn't it?

Which, of course, it is!

While I think of it, you might want to get a new Internet address for this new phone line, so that you can distinguish whether the sales inquiries are from your own web site, or from other people's pages.

Into a worldwide antique market

Operating worldwide becomes much more difficult but you can hardly avoid it since your new sales medium is cyberspace. Don't forget that your web site is now being "hit" by "surfers" from all around the globe and not just from within the U.S.A. So what happens if you sell that terrific music box to that dear old lady in Auckland, New Zealand? How do you get paid? How do you send it to her? What kind of Customs documentation does both the U.S. and New Zealand have? And last but not least, what kind of money will she pay you with?

Too much for you to handle? Of course not. Just remember how you went about getting the necessary information to set up this whole international business in the first place!

You're smart, you're adventurous, and you let your fingers do the walking. Call up the postal service, the U.S. Customs service, international airfreighters, FedEx, UPS, your bank, and anyone else that you can think off. Write all this information down, get all the brochures sent to you, set up an efficient filing system, and you will find it doesn't take a genius to be an international importer/exporter. It just takes hard work!

In a nutshell, this is how it works:

First. How do you get paid? In advance, that's how. Visa, MasterCard, American Express or by money order wired into your account. See! Easy, isn't it? But I don't know what the New Zealand Pound is worth! You don't have to. Ask them to pay you in dollars. What they pay their bank in N.Z. pounds is their business, not yours. But if you are curious, just buy any big city newspaper and check the financial section where they have a chart of currency conversions. Better still, look it up on the Internet.

Second. How do I send the goods? By air parcel post if it's

small and by airfreight if it's larger. Unless you are sending huge bookcases or armoires, you don't even have to bother with seafreight. Just remember this. Most shippers, be they the post office or commercial airfreight companies, will insist that you pay the freight up front. Doesn't that tell you something about the world? That means that you will have to find the freight charges out before finalizing the total price. Don't let the buyer pursuade you that they will pay these on receipt of the goods. You won't get it nine times out of ten. Am I too suspicious and jaded? Yes, don't forget that I've graduated from the school of hard knocks!

One other thing. Don't forget about insurance. When shipping overseas this becomes even more important. How the heck will you ever find the parcel once it's lost in New Delhi, India? Better you collect the insurance money and let the freight company worry about finding the goods to recover their losses.

Any other questions about becoming an international antiques dealer via the Internet?
I'm sure there are, but individual ones I can only answer via mail or via the Internet through my publisher.

Antique chat rooms

These abound by the hundreds and they are okay to play in when you have nothing else to do, which you shouldn't have, since you are too busy operating your booth, your Internet web site, and checking on your entries in other web pages. And that's not even considering all the packing and shipping that you have to do to cope with the new sales flooding in! Now you have no doubt why you married your better half, have you? Just don't forget to take him or her out to dinner once a week.

So how do these chat rooms operate? Log on, select one, type in a message and wait for a reply among all the chit chat that you see rolling across the screen, that's how.

From the above paragraph you'll see that I think that antique chat rooms are okay when you've nothing else to do, or when you need to get some information and are too lazy to run down a source. Someone in the chat room might just know the answer off-hand and you never know, you might strike it lucky and rustle up the person that desperately wants that antique ashtray that you just happen to have gathering dust. My advice is this: Log on to chat rooms sparingly, you have too much else to do in running your burgeoning cyberspace antique business.

Coping with the avalanche of information on the Internet

This section is easy. Why do you need to do anything when it's on the Internet and you can always punch it up with a few keystrokes? Just remember this piece of advice. You will never be able to remember everything. Just memorize how to operate the Internet and you will do okay. If it's a really important piece of information, file it electronically into an 'Information' folder where you can retrieve it at your convenience.

Protecting yourself on the Internet

"We've already covered this in chapter six and even elsewhere!"

Yes, I know, but I think it's so important that I am going to remind you of it again. Remember, in today's electronic age an unscrupulous person can debit your account or credit card account, find out almost everything about you, and even cause you to no longer exist—in documentary form. It takes a great deal of effort to remedy any electronic mayhem. Just don't give out personal information unless it's in closing a sale and unless your gut tells you that the person requiring it is a genuine customer or supplier. The Internet is wonderful, but it's a world without restrictions or controls. What makes it possible for you to become an international importer/exporter of antiques from your living room corner makes it possible for the criminally inclined to become an international charlatan.

Okay, time to stop. That was a lot to absorb. If it's still confusing, I suggest that you re-read it again and then go to the library and check out books on the subject of web sites. There are enough of them to keep you busy for weeks. Just remember, selling on the Internet is a tool, not the mainstay of your antique business. That's customer relations and your booth display.

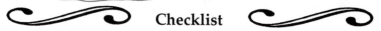 **Checklist**

- ❏ **Expanding your antique business**—open a second booth before all else. This is still your best bet when expanding your business. If this is too much, or even after you have done this, then expand on the Internet. You will have to do so in the future, anyway.
- ❏ **The technical feasibility of your own web site**—pay for one to get built by experts but follow my 15-point plan to ensure that your money is well spent.

❐ **What should your web site contain**—a KILLER title, clear and concise wording that grabs you with it's sparkle, and only minimum graphics with no background clutter or animation.

❐ **Servicing the U.S. market via your web site**—this is a huge leap in your expansion! You need a mini-warehouse operation with packaging, accurate record keeping, parcel service capability, and extra staff or a load of friends or children to help you.

❐ **Servicing the worldwide market via your web site**— even more of a leap with Customs documentation, air and sea freight requirements and financial transfers being essential for a smooth operation.

❐ **Antique chat rooms**—don't waste time in these. You've more profitable things to do in cyberspace.

❐ **Coping with the avalanche**—electronic record keeping is a must. This will require considerable effort to update. Pay your friend part time wages to take the load off your shoulders.

❐ **Protecting yourself on the web**—an essential reminder. The world is a dangerous place. Be careful!

Chapter 9

What's Up in the Traditional Antique Market?

What a change in three years!

I can't believe how fast three years have flown and how many changes have taken place in the antique business. Malls are bigger, better organized, full of entertainment, the Internet arrived in full force and antiques have even begun appearing in mainstream retail outlets.

Isn't it exciting? I think it is. Lord knows where the antique business is going with the world shrinking so fast! Now let's examine some of those changes.

Before we do that, I would like to take time out to thank all those wonderful people who came to my book signings, bought my books nationwide, and sent me such a load of wonderful letters in the last three years. I value you all, and may you be blessed with success.

Antiques in mainstream retail outlets

Antiques are no longer just being sold in the traditional way. In the last two years they have appeared in major retail stores, both furniture and general. This trend has come from Japan. I first saw it happening three years ago, although I wasn't sure whether it would take off in the United States, as it has in Europe.

Three years ago, on a buying trip in Wales, I stumbled over a Japanese lady purchasing container loads of antique furniture at one of my wholesalers. Since she was paying far higher prices than I could afford, I felt like a poor relation. My supplier was falling over himself in pampering to her requirements. After she had left, I talked to Jeff about her.

I was curious to find out how she operated her antique business in Japan as I wondered whether it had any application to the antiques business in the United States. "Oh, she sells her antiques through a chain of major department stores in Tokyo," he told me. "That's why she buys only the best and pays higher prices than any of my other customers."

Curious, I asked him more. "Yes, she rents space in a major retail store instead of in a mall," Jeff said, "and gives the store a percentage of her sales. This is good for both the store and my Japanese customer. She even buys building bricks from a demolished English cottage from me. Her Japanese customers buy them to build mantels and garden flower stands. "

Oh, the Japanese lady sells her antiques through a chain of major department stores in Tokyo.

It sure made sense to me. And why not? This lady was selling her antiques directly to the mainstream buying population while supplying unusual antiques such as old English bricks at the same time. No wonder she could afford such high prices! Major retailers get 'mungo' traffic through their outlets and traffic is the lifeblood of the antique retail trade.

"I wonder if the larger U.S. retailers are as forward thinking?" I thought.

On returning to Dallas, I asked around only to be looked at by merchandising managers as if I was a strange freak from Mars. They had never heard of such a thing and certainly wouldn't consider sub-letting retail floor space to an outside dealer.

That has all begun to change. Antiques, particularly furniture, are now entering the mainstream retail trade. For us booth holders that is both good and bad news. Good because it gives us new opportunities to expand by opening an outlet in a retail store ourselves, and bad because it brings increased competition to our buying and selling efforts. However, even this has a bright side.

$ $ $ $ $

To be sold in a major retail store with large overheads, the prices of antiques have to be higher and the volume has to be greater. One thing also is for sure, the quality definitely has to be higher.

As I said at the beginning of this book, 1998 and beyond will see a greater demand for quality in view of the fact that money is more available. Particularly when selling through a major retail outlet. A more **constant** standard of quality will also be required. This will mean that antiques being sold in major retail stores will require more effort to locate. Only the best will do.

So how does this new trend effect us, the ordinary dealer?

To our advantage I think. You do too? I knew you were a smart professional!

This trend of major retailers getting involved in antiques will effect us not only because it gives us new marketing opportunities, but since antiques are one off's, we can sharpen our buying, get better, unusual, and pretty products, charge higher prices, and make more profits! After all, major retailers have to charge more to cover higher overheads, thereby, giving us an opportunity to increase our prices also. In other words, we are taking advantage of market forces and competition prices to increase our profit levels.

Remember profit levels? We discussed them at the beginning of *Money from Antiques* in chapter four under 'type of merchandise'. They were business basics then and are even more important basics now. Just remember this: You are smart, up-to-date, nimble, and know your business inside out. Being unencumbered by bureaucracy, you can locate and purchase these quality antique pieces before the big stores even get off their butts! If you play your cards right and are bold and pushy, they will even use your expertise to help them stock their own operations. That way you can open a second business as an antique consultant. Go for it—where you take this new opportunity in the traditional market is up to you!

One other major trend in the antiques business that is worth watching is the one where mall owners are beginning to fill booths with their own merchandise, almost acting as competitors to private dealers. This trend, if it continues, has serious implications. How soon will it be before mall owners who now hold auctions on their own property start creaming off the best antiques for their own booths, and therefore, diminish the private booth holder's chances of competing? If this is happening in your mall, watch it very carefully. If it gets out of hand I suggest that you get out of that mall. Go elsewhere. I do not believe that mall owners can be both landlords and competitors. This makes their interests paramount. My question is this: Once a mall owner starts to do this, will he or she not spend the money allocated for promoting the mall to buy his or her own antique products? Of course he or she will. The mall's assets will go up to support bank and other loans. This is a bad trend started by malls that have empty space due to them not putting in enough effort to attract both customers and new dealers. If your mall is doing this, be careful and don't end up on the losing end. Locked into a long term lease while competing against your landlord for customers is a recipe for disaster.

Auctioning trends

Auctioneers are not my favorite people. Oh, I don't mean those wonderful, honest ones that are **established,** treat you right, are honorable, and back up their word with deeds. No, I mean all those fly-by-night ones that are flooding into the auctioneering business in droves. Unfortunately most of them are latching onto the antiques business, although the same is happening in the **computer** auctioning sector as well. One thing I learned from personal experience. In some states, such as Arkansas, there isn't even a requirement to put down a bond to get an auctioning license. At least that was the situation early in 1997. In Texas, there is at least a bond requirement with a state licensing procedure in place to air grievances. If you are using an auctioneer to buy or sell antiques this is what to watch out for: Check if the auctioneer's license is held by the owner, for how long, and ask to see it. A trend in the Dallas/Fort Worth area is that the owner of the business hires an auctioneer for one day only. In this way, the auctioneer is not responsible for paying you the money for your goods because he was only hired to conduct the actual sales.

Some unscrupulous businessmen are changing their names and auctioneers every three months and not paying customers for their consigned goods. While this is the exception rather than the rule, it is definitely on the increase. I know. It happened to me. Be warned!

In view of the above, I am sure that you can guess what my recommendations are. Only deal with well established auctioneers, ask to see their license, and shy away from consigning them your goods if you have any doubts at all. Having said that,

That special antique that the customer wants desperately.

I know auctioneers whom I trust and who do a great job. Use them, they are an essential supplier in the antiques business and deserve your support.

Warnings!

Two disturbing trends that have appeared in the business these past three years.

1: The prevalence of reproductions of all kinds flooding the market.

2: The number of malls that are turning into consignment stores.

Reproductions

So many reproductions are beginning to flood the market that it's getting to be a problem of major proportions, particularly in regard to ceramics. The Chinese manufacturers seem to have perfected the art of making their figurines, vases, and fruit and flower bowls look very authentic. Copies of most Messien pottery is now flooding the market in reproduction form. On a recent trip to Europe I saw shipping container after shipping container of reproduction Staffordshire and Winton ceramics. The quality of the reproductions was so good that even an expert would have difficulty in distinguishing the difference if some of these pieces were mixed in with other genuine antiques. This flooding of the market with such reproductions is a real problem as one has to be doubly careful at flea markets. Thorough checking takes time when you are trying to cover a lot of stands in as short a time as possible.

Reproduction antique furniture is still around in quantity, although shipments of the Far Eastern stuff seem to have reached a peak. The trend now in reproduction furniture, if you are going to buy it, is in the better European examples. Just remember that unless you have a very large booth with lots of space available, it is better to stick to genuine antique furniture only, and leave the reproduction to someone else. If by chance you do get a piece that is reproduction, mark it clearly so that the customer doesn't get confused. It will save you considerable embarrassment later on.

While we are on reproductions, be very careful of reproduction paintings. Even real experts are having trouble distinguishing between the real thing and the fake when it comes to old masters. Even some of the top auction houses have had a problem. One of the top two in the world was in the news this past year for inadvertently selling reproductions instead of the real thing. These people are the very top experts and it indicates how widespread this problem has become. If they can be fooled, what chance do we have?

Even the old give-aways no longer apply. The frames and backing that seemed to be a good indication of whether the painting was a genuine article in the past are now also being reproduced perfectly. Unless you know what you are doing I suggest that you avoid dealing in expensive paintings altogether. If you don't beware, it could cost you your shirt!

Malls turning into consignment stores

Three years ago I said that as the antiques market stabilizes and a shake-out takes place, a lot of the marginal malls will go out of business. That has proved to be the case. What I couldn't foresee at the time was that some of these malls would turn to being consignment goods stores. The problem with this, for you as a successful antique dealer, is that this retrograde trend continues today. As an example I will tell you about a mall that used to sell my books. Part of a company that successfully operated an antique mall in another area of Dallas, they opened a new location in a nearby city. It was huge—one of those the size of a large, large grocery store, which is exactly what the premises were before. The owners spent a ton of money refurbishing the place and opened this new location with great fanfare. The thing that disturbed me when I first went there was that the surrounding area was a middle to lower class working suburb. The amount of money spent on this mall didn't justify the type of grand operation they were setting up, although their contention that they would draw from rich neighborhoods around had some validity.

At first the mall filled up with antique booths. After 6 months, some of these were empty. That's when I moved my booth to another mall. Another six months went by and suddenly they lowered the booth rent in one part of the mall and let craft dealers in. Now I've nothing against crafts, but they don't belong in a mall with high-end antiques. Two years later, this grand antique mall is a consignment store with used clothes, secondhand radios and TV's and even second hand shoes being displayed in the booths. Now there's nothing wrong with the owners having to make it a viable business, it's just that those dealers that were locked into long term leases lost a lot of money over the last 12 months.

But that won't happen to you, will it? That's right. Being an antique professional now, you are keeping your eyes and ears open and instead of renewing your lease when you see the first drop in booth standards in your up-to-now successful mall, you are going to insist on only a month to month lease or at the most a three-month one. If the mall owner values your customers, he will agree to your request. If not, move your booth to a far safer location, despite all the hassle that this entails. It's your money, after all!

Marketing with new technology

This is an interesting trend in the antiques business. One that I am watching with interest.

Remember when we talked about selling advertising space on your web page in the previous chapter? You do? Great! Seriously, even though my comments may sometimes sound flippant, I don't mean to be. I really do have your best interest at heart and want you to succeed. It's that so much is changing in the antique business so fast that I am always sorry for those folks that don't seem to change with it and go out of business. I just don't want that to be you. I value everyone interested in the antique business, not just because you are a potential customer for my book, but also because I like the business and the genuine people in it.

Okay, back to advertising on your web site.

If that bank or mortgage company wants to advertise on your site, why don't you strike a deal to advertise your antiques at their branches or on their main premises. How about getting permission to place your very, very, tasteful brochures on the desk where their customers write out their checks? You know the one, the one that is in the middle of the room with a dozen pens that don't work connected to the table by silver chains!

And how about this for another great idea.

In our Dallas/Fort Worth area there are a number of large pre-owned vehicle mega-malls starting up. You've seen them on TV. The huge Auto Nation ones with a completely new way of selling used vehicles. If by chance you haven't seen one of their locations, go visit. They have rows and rows of computers in a very pleasant main hall. If you need a car you simply go to a computer screen, punch in all the details—model, year, color, option package, etc.—that you are looking for. In seconds the computer will throw out all the examples they have. The price, where they are located on their vast lot, and the salesman that will take you

Well displayed quality antiques.

directly to the car is all on the screen. No sales pressure, no confusion—you are in charge, and it works! That's my way of buying a car, not antiques. Antiques need experts to guide the customer. Cars we can purchase ourselves, thank you!

So how about you exchanging advertisements with one of these mega pre-owned car dealers? Why don't you ask if they will let you place a small advertisement on their computer screens in exchange for you placing theirs on your web site. Antiques and cars are both high priced quality items bought by people with considerable disposable income after all!

See my point?

"Same customer segment."

Right! You've got it.

But that isn't all you can do. Since you are selling space on your own web site, how about exchanging space on the bank's computerized system? Or on other web sites? Like on those belonging to realtors, those selling electronics, or boats, or women's fashions? The list is endless.

I know, I know, you're getting totally confused. "What has all this got to do with antiques?" I can hear you ask.

Here's what. It's all the same computer technology. You know what they say—this is the age of a new revolution! And it is. All your information can be downloaded onto a disk, mailed, downloaded into another system and hey presto! Your advertisement is on that bank's screens before you can say "By golly!" If you can get their passwords or codes, you can even download it on to their sites directly from your own computer but I very much doubt that they will even consider this. In fact, I know they won't. Not unless you have a very, very, good relationship with the manager. In that case you are probably their best customer.

Before you can place your electronic advertisement on the bank's screen however, you will have to get the bank's president to agree to your proposal, clear it with a thousand other bank officers, agree on how to do it with their vice president of computer operations, and discuss procedures with the technicians that implement it all. While doing this you will have to pretend that you are extremely computer literate. Ah well, your brother-in-law who works with that computer company can take care of the details for you when the time comes, can't he?

$ $ $ $ $

Seriously, the technological age has made us break out of stereotype classifications.

Marketing with this new technology is all the rage and the knowledge is freely available. Do it. I'm sure you will.

Having talked so much in the preceding paragraphs about all the high tech stuff, I want to spend a few moments on the basics again. Just remember that nothing will ever replace the basic antique booth filled with well displayed, quality antiques, and in which the customer gets excellent service. That is the bread and butter of the antiques business. For many wonderful dealers it will be enough. And so it should be. They will make a great living, have fun, and enjoy themselves. But for those that are more adventurous and want a higher income, I highly recommend the new technology. It is transforming the antiques business just like the malls did five years ago. Use the Internet and all it's associated technology for increased success to make **more money from antiques.**

New product sources

I make no apology in telling you that new product sources are directly related to the introduction of all this new electronic technology sweeping our antiques world. Before I explain this in detail, let's go over the traditional ways of finding products for your antiques business. For those that may want more basic details, I would again recommend that you buy *Money from Antiques.*

Here I want to say a few words about that. Before I get criticized for plugging my first book too much, I want you to note that this book is a continuation, and not a repeat, of things I wrote then. In light of this, let us briefly review the traditional ways of sourcing antiques.

Auctions, newspaper advertisements, garage sales, other dealers, house clearance sales, antiques magazines and newspapers—all these are excellent sources for quality antiques. In addition, we now have the Internet. This in itself is a huge leap forward in helping you locate good, quality antiques.

On the Internet we have a whole new list of broker agents willing to find that special antique that our special customer desperately wants to buy. You will find lists of them on basic web pages. All you have to do is to log on and punch up the different sites.

Now your reach is global!   *(Prague)*

Just remember the logistics, particularly if you are not envisioning setting up an Internet buying and selling warehouse operation as we discussed in the previous chapters. To buy on the Internet is difficult unless you make payment and delivery arrangements beforehand. And while we are discussing arrangements, let us discuss hidden costs.

To get an agent in the U.S. or overseas to locate the antique that you are desperately seeking, for them to buy it for you, send it to you, and to ensure that it is in good condition when it arrives is going to cost money. No one does something for nothing, so my recommendation when using this new sourcing method is to restrict yourself to small accessories only. Forget the big, bulky furniture. It's far easier to pack a small clock into a strong box and to send it via air parcel post than it is to send a heavy wooden buffet by sea freight. That is unless you are set up to do it.

Here I would like to give you an example, since many readers will only have small one or two booth operations. I mention it because I think that anyone, no matter how big or small, can use this example of what I call my new method of "agent" sourcing.

$ $ $ $ $

In England, just outside of Lynham, is a farmer I know. He dabbles in antiques on the side and has a computer. Last year he got connected to the Internet so that his wife could send and receive e-mail from their daughter in Scotland. Apart from farming wheat, he also attends all the local antique auctions, particularly if they have any 'country style' products for sale. During one of my overseas trips he and I set up this deal: If he locates a small antique that might interest me, he buys it. That evening he sends me an e-mail describing it in detail. If I don't want it he sells it in his barn as normal. If I agree to have it, he air parcel posts it to me. I, in turn, send him lists of small accessories that I want him to locate. The reason this arrangement works well for both of us is that he packs anything I want in a small box for his local postman to pick up on his normal rounds. It doesn't cause him or his wife a lot of effort. That's the key. Such a sourcing arrangement has got to be easy to operate for both parties. Buying and shipping antiques with as little effort as possible is what makes this "agent" buying work.

New selling opportunities

Having detailed the above with regard to buying, why don't we turn that around and use the same method for selling?

Good idea, huh? After all that farmer friend of mine is always looking for good silverware and I've had that teapot sitting in my booth for two months now. How about me sending him an e-mail describing it in detail so that he can offer it to some of his regular weekend browsers that buy silverware for their London booths? Good business is a two way street after all!

Enough said. I think you have the idea of the flexibility required in operating an 'agent' buying situation, but just in case you don't, lets think about it for another minute. For those that are still confused about what to do, I'll go over a few specific points.

Changes in the traditional market

1. Nothing replaces the traditional way of selling, or buying, in the antiques business. Your local auctioneer, importer, the garage sales and newspaper ads are all important sources of product. Customers visiting your booth, even more so. The antique business is a highly personal one and you must never forget that. Don't forget the basics just because new technology dazzles you.

2. Purchasing or selling antiques through the use of computers is great. Allocate time to do this as it is now a very important part of the antique business.We have reached the end of another chapter. It was fun. Here are the highlights.

What a change in three years

A momentous time! The changes in the antique business have been both good and bad, but thankfully mainly good. Bigger malls are drawing in more business for their booth holders, they have become family entertainment centers, and many even hold auctions to supply their dealers and to give them an outlet for slower moving merchandise. Then there was the growth in the Internet antique business. This simply exploded in 1997, continues the pace in 1998, and is good for the business as a whole.

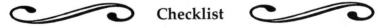 **Checklist**

❑ **What a change in three years!** —Larger malls, more entertainment and the Internet came roaring in to help the successful dealer become a more profitable businessman or businesswoman.

❑ **Antiques in mainstream retail outlets**—take advantage of this trend by selling your expert services or by renting space in their high traffic stores.

- ❑ **Auctioning trends**—don't use an auctioneer that changes his name every three months. Support your established one with his own permanent location.
- ❑ **Warnings!** —Reproductions are even harder to detect than before. Take care.
- ❑ **Malls turning into consignment stores**—if this is happening in your mall, get out of there as soon as you can—quicker if possible.
- ❑ **Marketing with new technology**—sell, buy, and swap advertising on other business's computerized programs.
- ❑ **New product sources**—build a relationship with broker agents to find that special piece for your good customers.
- ❑ **New selling opportunities**—use the same broker agents to sell that overstocked or slow moving silverware.
- ❑ **Changes in the traditional market**—nothing will replace good old customer service but try to grasp all this new technology to make even more money from antiques.

Chapter 10

$\mathcal{T}$ rends in Overseas Antique Markets

This is going to be a fun chapter and I'm looking forward to sharing all sorts of interesting information with you. For those dealers that haven't yet had the opportunity of traveling overseas, I will show you low cost ways of doing it. I personally love traveling and the antiques business is so popular and interesting in Europe that I think everyone should do it, at least once. For those who prefer to stay at home, but are interested in what's going on in England and Europe, I will tell you.

Trends effecting the antiques market in Europe, particularly England, have a very significant effect on what happens in the U.S. one or two years later. Much the same goes on in the fashion industry, where the haute-couture designs, so popular in France and Italy, become considerably modified ready to wear fashions in the U.S. the following year.

Before moving to specifics, I would like to cover just a few basic details. Since the United States is still a relatively young country, the supply of antiques is limited. Those that we have are so rare, that prices are astronomical and other than rich movie stars and corporate businessmen, most of us will never afford them. The Shaker antiques are an example. Hundreds of thousands of dollars are paid at auction for a very simple table or chairs. The same goes for traditional western antiques. With that in mind, the antiques that ordinary dealers are involved in are mainly from England, France and Argentina.

"That's strange! Why Argentina?"

Because a lot of German antiques ended up there, in view of Germany's connection with Argentina, before and after the second world war. Now they are being imported into the United States.

Certain towns are becoming major antiques centers. (Bath)

One has only to walk through an antiques mall today, to realize that most of the products filling the booths are of English origin.

"Won't they run out in England soon?" I have heard asked over and over again.

The answer is "Yes" but no time soon. Certainly not in our lifetime.

The reason is that the supply is governed by the growth of the housing industry in England, which in turn is controlled by very stringent city and local council by-laws. Getting land use changes is almost impossible, unlike here in America. The unintentional effect of this, is that antiques come on to the market in a very controlled and steady stream. This is not about to run out soon.

Enough about the background, let's see what's happening in the overseas antiques business.

Overseas trends

The antique business in Europe is going through a consolidation period. That trend will come here in 1998, so beware.

"What kind of consolidation?" all you smart antiques dealers are bound to ask.

Consolidation into specific locations, is the answer. In other words, certain towns and areas are becoming **major antique centers.** And this trend has accelerated in the last two years and continues to do so. An example of this, is an area around a town called Wootton Bassett that I used to visit. It's halfway down on the M4 to Wales. For those that would like to look it up on an English road map, Exit 16, on the London Cardiff motorway, I believe.

Wootton Bassett, when I first started buying antiques there, was a small town with three dealers. Product was cheap and good as the surrounding population was composed of rich farming types. Every little village around it also had a dealer or two. It was ideal for my buying purposes, as after visiting the three main street dealers in Wootten Bassett itself, I was able to cover the villages around it in an afternoon. Now, two years later, hardly any of those dealers are left. Why? Because they've all moved 15 miles down the road to Marlborough and Hungerford, the towns next to it.

$ $ $ $ $

What's this got to do with you in Grapevine, Texas, Bakersfield, California, or Sarasota, Florida? Very simply this. The same is happening here in the United States. Consolidation into centers developing as antique locations is taking place in the antique business in the U.S., just like in England.

"Why?" you may well ask.

Because as all the less efficient antique malls go under, all you smart dealers naturally gravitate to the better organized and bigger ones. This draws in customers who want the convenience of one-stop shopping. In turn, this draws in more landlords developing antique malls in that town or specific locality, which in turn, draws in more surrounding dealers, which in turn draws in more customers, and so on, and so on, and so forth.

The strange thing about this concentrating of dealerships, is that it seems to be following the trend in the restaurant and vehicle business. Haven't you noticed how the restaurants and car dealers all congregate in one place? It's good for business and draws in even more customers.

So what does this mean to you as an antiques dealer specifically?

It means that if you see Grapevine becoming a center for antiques, instead of Bedford or Euless, you should join the rush.

Move your booth five miles up the road when your lease is up. It's better to travel those extra miles to your booth if you are going to have twice the number of customers, isn't it? Only move before the rush of other dealers starts by taking my advice and watching the local trend. If you wait too long, the booth rents will go up in the new locations due to demand. Don't forget, the early bird catches the worm.

Before moving on to cover what else is happening in the antique business in Europe, and England in particular, I would just like to reiterate that this consolidation trend is very important for you to watch. Those dealers that don't and get left behind will lose a lot of money. Don't let that be you. That's why you bought this book. *"More Money from Antiques,"* means just that, doesn't it?

Specialization—It makes good business sense

Another trend developing in Europe, is that dealers are specializing more than ever.

As antiques, particularly good, quality ones, are getting more pricey, so dealers are taking advantage by specializing. This builds a booth's reputation for a particular type of merchandise. Silverware, antique watches, clocks and cigar items are all good examples of the types of product I'm talking about.

Country and rustic antiques are a must.

This specialization, in turn, draws in customers who already know what merchandise they are looking for and are therefore, not just lookers but serious buyers. I would recommend readers of this book to seriously consider specializing. Oh, I know, I know! Three years ago I said exactly the opposite. "Don't specialize, it restricts your customer base," I said then. Yes! But I also said: "Be flexible, go with the flow, and take advantage of hot trends, didn't I?" That's one thing about the antique business. It's in a constant state of flux. To succeed in this business, you have to be nimble on your feet.

Arrange garden antiques in your booth as if they were in a natural setting.

So what is my new recommendation?

Specialize for the next two years. Particularly in good quality and hard-to-find accessories. Then when the trend changes again, pick up on it early and change with it!

Country and rustic antiques a must!

The third, and just as important, trend taking place in the antique business in Europe is that 'country' or 'rustic' antiques are becoming immensely popular. This trend has been growing over the last five years, and I mentioned it in **Money from Antiques** three years ago. If anything, the market for rustic antiques has grown the quickest. I think it's because as we all have a bit more disposable income, we all have more time to think about the "good ole' days." It's either that, or we need a break from all this fast-paced technology that we are having such a difficult time absorbing, and rustic antiques in our homes does that for us.

My recommendation to you as a professional antique dealer is this: If you have a ready supply of 'country style' antiques, specialize in them. You can make a lot of money from this trend which I believe will continue for some time. Besides which, I like country and rustic antiques. There's something solid about them, as if they have seen life and are bemused by it all.

As if that isn't enough of a change effecting antique dealers in the United States, here is another. And this is one trend that I think is very, very, exciting. The reason for all my excitement is that this particular sector of the antique market is wide open.

So what is it?

It's the growing trend in using garden antiques, not just for garden purposes, but as interior decorative pieces as well.

Garden antiques—used for double purposes

The use of garden antiques for both interior and exterior decorating is a very exciting trend. Long used to being the poor relation and just a very, very, specialized business, garden antiques in Europe are coming into their own. And this trend is just at the beginning stages. It will roar into the antique business in the United States like a house on fire in the next few years, believe me. I see it already happening in Dallas and Houston, two towns on the forefront of the antiques business in Texas.

So what kind of garden antiques should you look for?

Well, how about concrete statues, fountains, metal foot scrapers, old horse-drawn carts, lots and lots of cast-iron railings (remember them?—the two I sold to that dealer from Atlanta that made them into a table by adding an oval glass top?), old antique water pumps, metal arbors, sun dials—the list goes on and on. It's endless. The older, more rusty, more chipped, and more distressed looking, the faster it sells! And if it has a green verdigris finish on it like you see on old brass, you won't even be able to put it in your booth before it is sold. I guarantee it.

All I can say, is that I like this trend. I always do when I feel especially excited about something in the antiques business that is catching on—particularly when it is still in it's infancy. For dealers just getting started, this trend would be worth specializing in right away.

$ $ $ $ $

And why is all this demand for garden antiques happening? Because as people are better off, they look to spending more money on their homes. With England and the United States expected to continue in an extended economically prosperous period, this trend for more expensive items will stay strong. And there's another reason. Garden antiques actually look terrific in sunrooms, entry halls, and large breakfast rooms. They give these areas a fresh and different look.

But there is one snag. I must mention it, before all you dealers jump into this new sector of the market.

Most garden antiques are large, heavy, or awkward to move around. To buy and sell them, you have to be organized, have a large truck, or know a handy mover that will do work for you when business is slack. Get it? When he is slack! That way **he** won't charge you the earth for moving a heavy, awkward load, and you won't pull your back helping him.

So what do you do with all these garden antiques? How do you display them? Show them off?

You arrange them in your booth like and you use lots of grape vines, flowers, and bush arrangements. Old rope, beat up milk cans, and even old bricks to decorate them make the whole display both interesting and wonderful to look at. Just make sure that you are prepared for the rush, because believe me this is the new hot, hot, hot, trend in the antiques business.

Okay, since you have been taking notice of what I've been saying, being the terrific antique dealer that you are, I will only go over the major points.

Consolidation of antique dealers into specific localities is underway. Consider this when renewing your booth lease. Do

One experiences how local English people live.

you want to stay in your town or area, or do you want to move your booth into the one in the nearby town that is developing a reputation for being an antiques location? While you are about it, is it time for you to specialize? You will make more money if you do, believe me. And while you are specializing, how about those country or garden antiques? If you are set up to handle them, have a large enough booth, or can get hold of a handy mover, this is the way to go. You will make a lot more money if you do, as I believe that this trend is here to stay.

European Antique Tours

You've heard me talking about the English antique scene and it makes your mouth water. What you would give to see it for yourself, many of you are thinking.

Well how about doing it? Too expensive? Not if you follow my advice.

For all those antique dealers who would dearly love to visit Europe but have never been able to because of cost, I have a number of suggestions which make it affordable. First, I would suggest that an initial European antique trip should be to England only. This is not just because I particularly like it there, but because the language, ease of traveling, prices of accommodation, and the concentration of antiques within short distances, all make it feasible for the first-time traveler.

Let's take the airfare for a start, since this is your single biggest cost. I am sure that I don't need to tell you that the best time of the year to travel is in the off-season. That means between late November to early March. Barring December 20th to 29th which is a very busy period, of course. During these months, all the major airlines reduce their rates considerably, particularly from January to March. American Airlines and British Airways had them down as low as $400 return in January 1998. Call up all the major

Inside a posh B&B.

airlines and find out who is the cheapest. The only thing that you must accept with low fares is that you must be flexible. Sticking to dates or times cost you money. Since you are your own boss with your own antiques business, changing travel dates at the last minute shouldn't be a problem, should it?

Ask the airlines for their very lowest fares and although the departure dates and times might be awkward, the trade off is in savings.

One other way of getting low fares is by surfing the Internet. Remember that electronic front of all information? Isn't it amazing how cyberspace has effected our lives? Before I digress back to airfares. Just punch up "airfares" on your web browser and you are going to be amazed at some of the offers that are being made on flights to England and Europe. Again, remember to be

England's splendid history.   *(Wales)*

flexible. It will save you money. And don't forget to pay by credit card. That way you may gain more air miles.

Now we come to transport at destination, whether by road or otherwise. This is the second biggest cost in an antique trip to England, and to save money, don't use a regular car rental company. They cost too much. Rather than using Hertz, Dollar or Alamo, use a small local car hire company, buy a season rail or bus ticket, or even a local tour ticket. In using train or tour bus transport, you save on the daily mileage charges, but lose out on flexibility.

I personally like the freedom of traveling without specific schedules, and to do this cheaply, road transport is necessary. I use a small car rental company called Simba Car Hire in Corsham, Wiltshire. Their phone number is Corsham 1225 810559 for those that are interested. They will pick you up at London or Gatwick airport for the cost of the rail fare, or if you are like me, you can catch a bus down to them at nominal cost to get acclimatized after your flight. It's actually quite fun watching the countryside whiz by after a ten-hour overnight flight. You can also snooze if you like. That way you will be fresh and ready to go as soon as you pick the car up. It also gets you out of the heavy traffic that is a feature of the London areas.

The third most expensive factor in an antique trip to England, is the cost of accommodation. As I mentioned in *Money from Antiques*, I do not stay in name brand hotels. They are far to expensive. Besides which, why stay with your fellow countrymen? Merge yourself into the foreign culture to really savor it, is my motto.

$ $ $ $ $

Bed and breakfasts are definitely the way to go to save money in England. At between 20 to 30 pounds ($35 to $50) for a double room, they are great value. Not only are bed and breakfasts in England clean and cheap, they all serve a wonderful breakfast that is worth at least 10 pounds ($17). Stuff yourself with cereal, eggs and bacon, toast and marmalade, as well as homemade scones, and save your lunch money. You'll be surprised how this will add up. It will also stop you gaining weight on your trip.

Bed and breakfasts are to be found everywhere in England, Scotland and Wales. Just check the small signs on the roadside, or consult a bed and breakfast guide that you can get at any bookstore. Every village or town has them. Many pubs also rent rooms overnight. I personally never plan ahead and just start looking for a B&B in the afternoon as I drive along. This may not suit everyone, but I like the spontaneity of it all, and the thrill of finding somewhere new that has it's own characteristics.

Staying in bed and breakfasts, rather than in hotels, has another advantage to my way of thinking. One experiences how local English people live. This can be fun and you can develop some really long lasting friendships in this way. Not only are these friendships good for your soul, they're also good for business. Your new friends can always buy local antiques for you or you can even swap homes with them for vacations, can't you?

Now we come to the last major cost of a trip to England. It is the cost of food. It simply does not make sense to save money on airfares, transport, and accommodation, just to lose all those savings by eating in restaurants where the cost of a meal is the same as the cost of your accommodation, is it now? So eat in pubs, or buy food at a grocery store and eat it in a park, by the village pond, or in your room. The B&B's don't mind. And many of the large English supermarket chains, like Tescos, now have cafeterias in the grocery store themselves. These are self-service, cheap, and serve excellent food. Just remember that the grocery stores are not open 24 hours like here in America. Most close at about 10 PM, but this varies from town to town. Why does it vary so? Because each town or area has historically enacted by-laws that were originally decided by the local Lord or dignitary. Some of these by-laws stretch way back in history to William the Conqueror. Quaint isn't it?

$ $ $ $ $

All of the above advice on saving money is no use unless you get organized in advance and plan your trip in a systematic way. The best way to do this, is to use a motorway as the spine for your English trip. In that way, you can get a rail ticket and get off at different towns enroute to a major city that will be your turn-around point. If traveling by car, the same applies.

All this theory is okay, but how does it work in practice? To show you, here is a trip that I do often. It takes 9 or 10 days depending on how I feel, and costs me less than $1,000 in total, inclusive of airfare. That's for a single person. For double it has cost me less than $1,800. The extra cost is mainly due to food, one extra air ticket, and slightly better, and even some posh B&B's.

I always plan to start my trip on a Thursday or Friday, which allows me a first weekend of antique shopping at all the car boot sales (flea markets—in American parlance). Thinking about the $1,000 reminds me that it's not much more than the return airfare from Dallas to San Francisco to see my son, which is only half the distance. Good value, this trip to England, isn't it?

Importation regulations

Having sold you on taking a buying trip to England, how about the regulations for bringing antiques back into the United States? Basically, there are very few. I recommend that first-time buyers stick to small accessories only. These can be packed into sturdy boxes and be brought back with you as unaccompanied baggage on the same flight that you travel on. Keep a running list as you buy, and all the receipts for Customs. That way you can pay the duty on arrival. You can also clear them by spending an extra half hour at the airport, and save yourself the cost of a clearing agent. At last count, the duty you have to pay on the total is 10%, so this is worthwhile. If, however, you buy more than $1,500 you will need a clearing agent to do it for you. This will add at least $400 to your costs to cover his fee.

Freight

Let's cover that here. Unless you are talking about importing container loads or large pieces of furniture, we are talking specifically about airfreight. This is relatively inexpensive for standard-sized boxes. If I were you, I would check with UPS on their rates,

Slovakia and Poland have antiques, but they are very hard to find.

as they have become the major player in airfreight from the United Kingdom. While you are about it, also check their airfares, as they now carry a few passengers in their cargo planes in a small cabin section. They might give you a deal you can't refuse for both the trip and the freight! That would be a first, wouldn't it?

Letters of credit

I would like to mention these for those dealers interested in bringing larger shipments of antiques from overseas. International Letters of Credit are used just like local ones. They promise to pay the supplier on presentation of all the documents indicating that they have delivered the goods to a shipper for onward transport to you. Notice that I said indicating. L/C's do **not** guarantee that the goods shipped are as ordered. It's something that a lot of dealers forget, and therefore, you have to trust the supplier to load what you ordered. The best assurance of getting exactly what you ordered is always to see the shipment loaded, even if it costs you to stay a few extra days.

Customs regulations

I briefly mentioned these earlier on, but I have included this small section because I think that all antiques dealers, large or small, should familiarize themselves with the Customs regulations. The best way to do this is to call up your local U.S. Customs Office and ask for a briefing. The officers are always very helpful and obliging. Briefly, the Customs regulations governing antiques are as follows: Over 100 years old, and there is no duty to pay on imported antiques. If the piece is less than 100 years old, then there is an 8 percent duty to pay. So why the extra 2% when the antiques travel with you as unaccompanied baggage? Because for ease of documentation in the rush to clear passengers through Customs, the Customs department at the airport rounds out the figures.

Currency

Since this chapter is about traveling overseas to familiarize oneself with the English antique business, and also to hopefully buy a few, I would like to talk briefly about money. Is it best to carry dollars, buy pounds, travelers checks, or drafts? I personally prefer just to carry dollars. I can change them at any High Street bank in any English town, as and when I need to. That way, if I don't spend all my money, I don't have to pay a double exchange transaction fee. Just be certain that you keep your cash safe. I always, always, carry it in a zippered inside jacket pocket. That way I can feel that it is still there. Peeling off a few bills to carry in my wallet also ensures that I am not flashing a lot of cash around when I am haggling with a dealer over that antique cigar lighter in the Hungerford town hall on a Saturday morning.

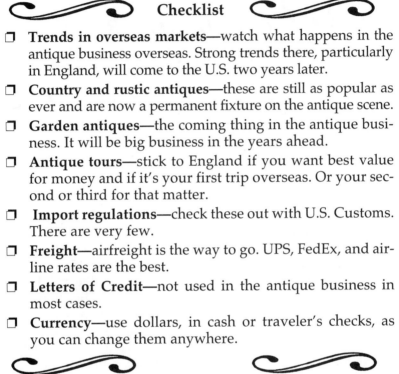

Checklist

- ❐ **Trends in overseas markets**—watch what happens in the antique business overseas. Strong trends there, particularly in England, will come to the U.S. two years later.
- ❐ **Country and rustic antiques**—these are still as popular as ever and are now a permanent fixture on the antique scene.
- ❐ **Garden antiques**—the coming thing in the antique business. It will be big business in the years ahead.
- ❐ **Antique tours**—stick to England if you want best value for money and if it's your first trip overseas. Or your second or third for that matter.
- ❐ **Import regulations**—check these out with U.S. Customs. There are very few.
- ❐ **Freight**—airfreight is the way to go. UPS, FedEx, and airline rates are the best.
- ❐ **Letters of Credit**—not used in the antique business in most cases.
- ❐ **Currency**—use dollars, in cash or traveler's checks, as you can change them anywhere.

It's the end of the chapter again, but we are staying with the overseas theme in the following one. Don't go away. After that, we'll have to come back down to earth. It's been fun. Stay with me and let's have more.

Chapter 11

*C*omprehensive Review of the Antique Market

The antique business is in constant flux, expanding, contracting, and re-shaping itself at an incredible rate.

Why is this? Because it is a business that most people without extensive training or financial resources can get into. A little drive and initiative will do it. In other words, the antique business is an every-man's or woman's business. It is also an interesting and fascinating business, because all of us like stability and history, let alone to make money. Not only that, but the antique business automatically involves products that come mainly from Europe and in themselves have a historical background. This is fascinating. After all, we only have to think of how antique products evolved to be captivated. The hall tree is an example.

If you really think about it, what other furniture item serves such a useful purpose as a halltree? Where else would we hang a coat, or hat, or be able to put a pair of muddy shoes, or leave our wet umbrella when coming out of the rain? No, a halltree is not just a useful item that has evolved through time, but it is also a good looking piece of furniture that has evolved into an interesting conversation piece. It is also an antique that we can make money on. And that surely is the main purpose for us being in the antique business, is it not?

Enough of the waxing lyrical and let's get on with seeing what direction the antiques business is taking, both here in the United States and overseas.

The present

Having observed the antiques business closely for nearly ten years, both here and overseas, I believe that the antiques

What other furniture item deserves such a useful purpose as a halltree?

business has come of age. It has matured, become a far more professional business, and requires a lot more planning and awareness than it did a few years ago. What does all that mean to the present day antique dealer? I believe that it means that to prosper in today's climate we all have to become far more professional at our chosen business. And what does professional really mean? It means that more than ever that we have to make the customer feel that they are number one.

That means that we have to offer free delivery within a certain area, our booth presentation has to be better, we have to market our products rather than waiting for customers to walk into our booth, we have to watch the population make-up of our location, and having done all that, we have to cater to the specific requirements of our captive customer base. If we don't do it all, we will go out of business, just like some of the less professional malls and dealers are doing right now.

The future

Having said all the above, what do I think will happen in the antique business in the next few years, you may well ask.

Okay, at the risk of sticking my neck out, and after consulting my crystal ball, here goes. I believe that the antique business will require even **more** professionalism from its dealers in the next few years.

"Darn," I can already hear you saying. "I thought that having got set up I could sit back a little and just make money!"

Yes, I know. I wish it for you too, but it's not going to happen. Not unless you become a real businessman or businesswoman. And there's the rub.

$ $ $ $ $

Unlike a few years ago, when the antiques business was growing by leaps and bounds, it has slowed down to a more normal rate of growth, about 8 percent I estimate. That means that dealers are all going to have to take care of every single customer, no matter what. We will also have to operate more like traditional businesses than like something we can do by the seat of our pants.

Those that do, will prosper, those that don't will fall by the wayside. In other words, I think that a shake-out among dealers is imminent. And it will be a big one. So what changes will good dealers have to make to prosper in the future? Well, for a start, they will offer free delivery within a specified area and delivery at cost to an area encompassing the whole of their city or county. Sound too much? Well consider this! You have a customer that wants to buy that dining table set for their mother who lives 30 miles away. Are you going to lose the sale and the $1000 in your bank account, or are you going to charge them $30 and spend one afternoon delivering it out of town? You are going to deliver it, I bet. If not, you won't be in business for too much longer.

Being professional also means that we are going to have to be aware of what is going on in the antique business and watch it far more closely. We are going to have to read fashion magazines, take note of what's going on in the furniture business, and listen far more closely to our customer's requests. Furthermore, we are going to have to become professional **retailers,** rather than antique dealers. That means that we are going to have to operate an antique business as a total package and offer service above and beyond just selling a piece out of our booth or store. And the way we will do this will be by increasing our add-on sales.

Add-on sales? Yes. Successful antique dealers are going to build relationships with interior decorators, fabric stores, house painters and even carpet suppliers. I have seen this happening in Europe and you can bet that it will come here.

If all the above sounds confusing and too much work, let me give you an example of how this works in real life.

$ $ $ $ $

I know a lady antique dealer in England that started with a higher end antique booth in a mall some four years ago. As her business grew she concentrated on better and better quality products. Two years ago her sales leveled off. On one of her deliveries the customer happened to mention that she was wanting to re-paint the room into which that corner table was going. Quick as a flash my friend offered to arrange the re-painting for her as she knew a painter that lived on the same street as she did. One week later the paint job was done, my friend had collected a ten percent commission from the painter, and she was discussing the drapes with a drape supplier and the delighted customer. Now my friend has a different business. She is a consultant in which antique sales are part of the whole concept. When I last talked to her, she had two green vans with gold lettering on them, called her business by some fancy sounding name, and was delivering two very expensive writing desks. The customer she was going to visit was also changing out the baby's room to fit the antique sleigh bed that my friend had sold her. The other purpose for my friend's visit that morning was to meet with the painter, the carpet supplier, and the customer, to discuss the possible changes to the large reception area.

Get the picture? Increased service has led to an expansion in her basic antique business. But back to my review.

In the previous chapter I talked about my excitement at the growing trend in garden antiques and its future effect on our wonderful business. In the same manner, I notice the same thing happening here already, only this time with antique western items. Such as what? Well, such as horse drawn carts, old sweat stained sombreros, antique saddles and harnesses, and antique farm implements. Oh, I know that there has always been a small segment of the market dealing in such items, but with the proliferation of Mexican-style restaurants, demand for such western antiques is rising to an all-time high. For those dealers not yet taking advantage of this trend, I recommend that you do. It will add valuable sales to your business.

Here's an aside. How many of you know that old second-hand Levi's are fetching astronomical prices? It seems that the Japanese have an insatiable appetite for them—the older and more worn the better—as long as they are the old genuine "Made in America" article, not one of those made in Thailand or Madagascar, as so many things are these days.

At this stage, I would like to take time out and review the English antique market a little more, as it has such a great effect on what will happen in our own antique businesses in the years ahead.

Review of the English antique market

English antiques are going to get more expensive and in shorter supply. That means prices are going to rise at our own auctions, since 80 percent of the antiques being sold here come from England and France. Plan for it, prepare for it, and start to sell off your cheaper antiques to stock up with more expensive and better quality ones now. Don't wait. Prices will go up, believe me. Think of it as money in the bank and remember, the early bird catches the worm.

$ $ $ $ $

Rents in antique malls are also beginning to rise in England. This is starting to worry dealers there, and they are handling it in different ways. Some are simply getting out of the business altogether, others are setting up their own full-service stores, and others are getting together, forming their own corporations, and becoming mall owners in their own right. For those of you that have a strong dealer association, this might be the way to go. It definitely controls your overheads in a more stabilized manner.

In reviewing the English antique scene on a recent trip, I was struck by the fact that it is a very much a more solid business than it was five years ago. The different antique products have developed into almost their own specialized sectors, rather than being part of a pretty disparate and diverse overall scene. This is most obvious when you go into malls such as the Gray's Antique Mall just off Old Bond Street in London. Here the booths have all turned to antique jewelry and the lines of new BMW's and Jaguars parked outside bear out that this is proving successful. Consolidation, seems to be the watch word in Europe. I believe that the same will happen here as I mentioned before.

Weekend antique markets have also become a big thing. Now I'm not talking about flea markets, but actual **markets** with only good quality antique products. Dealers are combining their resources, hiring a town hall, and adding to their booth sales by holding an all weekend "event". This holding of "sales events" is gathering strength and most larger villages have one at least once a month in winter and twice a month in summer. So how will these market trends in Europe affect us?

Review of the U.S. antique market

Expect a shake-out in our market. It is already underway. Mall locations and specialization is going to be of crucial importance to both new and established antique dealers. But there is even more money to be made if you become a 'whole' antique business, rather than just an ordinary one. Offer ancillary services to draw in customers wanting a complete package rather than just selling them that corner writing desk.

Isn't it amazing what people are specializing in now? Antique chimney pieces, bathroom fittings, embroideries, military items, kitchenalia, (a term now used in England) textiles, wine bin labels, champagne taps, antique maps, wines, work tools, art deco, antique breweriania (?) and even medical, dental and pharmaceutical antiques—all have specialist antique dealers throughout England.

But what relevance does this have to an ordinary booth holder doing reasonably well in an established mall in the United States?

Well how about setting up a corner area for a terrifically presented antique map section?

Just imagine how interesting this could be if you had antique maritime charts, maps, old sextants and world globes? Add some books on maritime subjects, some old ship models, set up spotlights to illuminate the corner brightly, add a few signal flags at the back, and you have a section that will attract

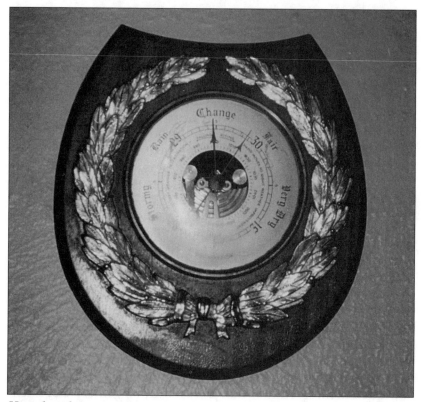

How about barometers?

men to your booth who will want some of the items for their dens. It will also attract their wives or girlfriends who will buy that accessory table for the new addition to their home.

Buyer and supplier lists

How does one find suppliers and even buyers for all these specialized antiques? Well, how about trying the Internet for a start. And don't just look for suppliers or buyers who advertise! Look for web sites with antique newspapers, magazines, and catalogues as well. That way, on a quiet Monday in your mall, you can go through them, note their mailing addresses and send postcards requesting trial copies in which details of suppliers and buyers are listed. All it takes is work, after all. You have to be like a detective, or a ferret, to build up your specialist suppliers and customers. It's a critical part of your business, and deserving of extensive effort.

Antique magazines in particular are great sources of special-

Barometers and corkscrews.

ized products. More so in England than in the United States. For example: *The Collector* is a monthly magazine published by Barrington Press in Uxbridge, London, that lists over 50 pages of specialist suppliers and buyers together with lists of antique fairs and exhibitions every month. Here in the U.S., Antique Trader Publications publish the *Antique Trader Weekly* which does just a terrific job in the same specialized antiques. Buy it—knowledge is part of being one step ahead in a successful antiques business.

Mail order

I have put this section in here, because I have noticed that many dealers in Europe actively promote mail order to increase their business. They do this by placing very small and cheap advertisements in local and regional newspapers covering areas in distant parts of the country. Very often these local or small country papers are owned by one group and you can get a group rate to cover a dozen papers at one time. This is a good way of getting not just more buyers, but also new suppliers, particularly if you advertise that you both buy and sell antiques. I think more dealers should avail themselves of the cheaper advertising rates in these local papers to spread their customer base.

So how relevant is all the above to your small antique business?

As I have said before, it all boils down to antique dealers now having to work that much harder to keep expanding their businesses. It's simply no longer feasible to grow by just catering to walk-in customers only.

So how about becoming even more professional in your business in the next few years?

It'll be fun, but harder work, to make even more money from antiques. Just think of it like this. All the harder work will result in more income and will be well worth it, I promise. Having expanded on events overseas, I shall summarize everything and then it's time to cover more basic matters.

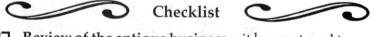 **Checklist**

- ❏ **Review of the antique business**—it has matured tremendously in the last three years and to succeed, dealers are going to have to offer more services.
- ❏ **The future**—dealers should build relationships with painters, carpet suppliers, and interior decorators to offer a "whole" package. It will make them more profitable.
- ❏ **The English antiques market**—antiques are getting more expensive in England and dealers are both consolidating and specializing.
- ❏ **Review of the U.S. market**—a shake out is underway and service will help you prosper. Specializing is the way for dealers to go.
- ❏ **English suppliers**—get catalogs and publications to run down specialized suppliers for your new displays. These are advertised on the Internet.

- ☐ **Mail order**—dealers should build this sector of their business up as it adds valuable profits to the bottom line.
- ☐ **The effect of the changes on you as the dealer**—successful dealers can no longer rely on walk-in trade alone to grow and prosper. They will have to become aggressive marketers of specialized antique products.

Chapter eleven is at an end. It summarized what dealers will have to look out for and do to make even more money from antiques. Let's now look ahead and combine the new with the old, shall we?

Chapter 12

The New and the Old for the Best Antiques Business

Combining the new with the proven old is the best way to run a successful antiques business in 1998 and beyond. This may sound like a simple statement, but just remember that only two years ago the Internet was not as all-encompassing as it is today. The very thought that we now have a worldwide customer and supply base for just a few dollars a month can be very overpowering, but we must not forget the fundamentals of the antiques business, or else it will come back to haunt us. Thinking about this statement reminds me of someone I was talking to just before Christmas. This lady was telling me that as 1997 was closing out, she set herself a priority of changing many aspects of her life. Her reasoning was that to make decisions on the new directions she wanted in her life she had to set deadlines and cut off some of the things that seemed to continue without much change. My answer was: "Why throw out the baby with the bath water? Why not keep some of the stability and add the new intentions to ensure that you don't lose it all?"

The same applies to the antique business. All dealers should constantly review their operations, delete what isn't working, try something new, and build on the proven basics.

So how does an antique dealer combine the new with the old?

Well, let's take the old first. Let's update it in light of the new trends we have talked about.

First thing we have to do is to put far more effort into presentation in our booth or booths. We all tend to get lax and now is the time to renew our enthusiasm for this vital chore. Remember me talking about painting a scene on the back wall of your booth? And how about that wine barrel gathering dust at the back? And that railing that you have leaning against the wall in the garage at home? And what else have we got? Well, we've got all those antiques being advertised by that broker on the Internet web site, haven't we?

Okay, here's what we should do. We roll up our sleeves, decide that tomorrow is usually a slow day, and then do the following:

Late tonight or first thing tomorrow, we will go to our wallpaper store or major hardware warehouse and buy wallpaper depicting an 'olde worlde' scene. You know the type—horses, carriages, ladies with parasols, and the odd dalmatian running around.

While we are about it, we will also buy a poster stand and large plastic backboard at the crafts store. They all have them. Next we will do the following: Tonight, we will get onto the Internet and print the specifications and pictures of some of those antiques that the broker is advertising, the unusual ones that come with complete details. Even better, if we happen to have two computers at home, and if one is an old one that still has sufficient RAM and can get the Internet but doesn't have all the bells and whistles, we shall bring that down to our booth with us.

$ $ $ $ $

Now we have all the pieces in place. Combining the new with the old—that's our objective. First we will stick up that new wallpaper. Already the booth looks different. Next let's stand up that old railing in the corner and the wine barrel in the front just by your booth dividing wall. Get out all those accent pictures of horses and fox hunts that we haven't been able to sell and hang them on the metal railing. Group them all together, but not in even rows. We want the display to look spontaneous and interesting. Next we shall arrange the buffet in the other corner and stand the posterboard on its tripod beside it. If you are one of those dealers with that old computer, set that up on the buffet also. Above this arrangement, display a banner that says: "Worldwide antique locating service."

Are you getting the picture?

Now rearrange some more product in the booth. No, not that stuff that was there before! Put in the inventory that was in your garage, at least enough of it to make the booth look completely different, to have a new look so to speak. Over in the corner where you hung the horse pictures, put up a tasteful sign that says "Western antiques available by special order." If you have

Remember how flowers add color and interest?

some old harnesses, drape these around the railing as well. And
that antique horse collar makes a great frame for your business
name plaque with your phone number on it.

Now back to the posterboard. Pin some of those antique pictures that you down loaded off the Internet on it, print out some
extra ones, stack these extra copies on the buffet—making sure
that you have put your business address on them— and if you
have that old computer, switch it on, leaving the screen saver on
until you need to access the Internet to find that old gentleman
what he specifically needs so desperately. Now throw a bunch of
flower arrangements around (remember how vital they are to
add color and interest?), drape some grapevines around (Don't
tell me you've forgotten how effective they are?) and you are in
business again. Now your booth looks new, different, and fresh.

While you are doing this change out have you noticed the
other dealers flocking around asking you to look up a supplier
for blue and green 1880 widgets for them? Oh, before you for-

get, chain down the computer. Drill a little hole in the case and chain it down so that it doesn't develop legs. If you don't it'll walk, I promise you. Even antique dealers are not all honest. One other thing, get a computer lock fitted so that people aren't switching it on when you are not around and using it without paying for your new "Locating" service.

So what kind of antique business have you got now?

Well, you have one that stands out as being very, very professionally run. Not only that, but you have combined the new with the old. One word of caution here. To fully utilize what you have done, you will have to work a lot harder. It will even mean that your significant other cannot sit at home on that Saturday afternoon, he/she will have to help you deal with customers, either on the net or as head salesman in your booth.

But there's still more you can do. Remember that posterboard notice? How about another one detailing your "Total package services"—the ones where you and the interior decorator, the painter, and the carpet salesman all go together to the lady's house to advise her on which antiques she needs, what color scheme is suitable for that new reception area, what drapes will highlight the windows, and what color of carpet will set off the whole ensemble? Revamping that customer's dreary reception room will bring you lots of profit, believe me. I actually saw this very situation personally, so that's how I know it works.

$ $ $ $ $

It was some time ago. I was delivering an antique bookcase to a customer in Plano, a wealthy suburb of Dallas. The painter, the carpet supplier, and the drape salesman were all there giving advice and finalizing orders. With three people around, the customer didn't haggle over prices, it would have been too embarrassing. I was the only one who didn't make any extra profit that day. I had given the lady a discount in the store and had even delivered the piece free. If I had been in charge of the whole operation I would have gotten her better prices and made myself ten percent commission. I would also have had a grateful customer for life!

So what have we done in combining the new with the old?

We changed our business from being just another antiques booth to being a professionally run total operation, that's what. We added the Internet, a specialized corner to keep up with trends, introduced a far higher level of service, and even started a consulting service for other dealers! All this will increase our income considerably. The only negative? We have to work that much harder. And if we don't have help, how about combining our operation with our neighboring booth holder?

Knock down the intervening wall, get her/him to work as hard as you at displaying goods more professionally, and then share the hours now required to operate this thoroughly modern antiques business. Just one major detail. Finalize how much he/she will get in sharing the work with you or whether her payoff is the use of the Internet. Make sure that all the financial details are nailed down at the beginning of your partnership and get them down in writing. The same goes for your agreement with the interior decorator, the painter and the carpet supplier. Just a simple hand written agreement will do. Things can get messy if you don't write it all down and I am talking from experience, believe me.

In finalizing this section, I would like to offer another word of encouragement to you.

$ $ $ $ $

Just remember, it may all sound like a lot of work to combine the old with the new, but it's not. Once you have the new additions set up, it becomes surprisingly easy to operate. Not only will all these new services increase your income considerably, but the work required will fill in those quiet, boring periods when business is slow. That will make you the only antique dealer working hard to keep up, when all others are sitting staring into space and worrying how bad business is. You will have so much to run down on the Internet that you won't have the time to get bored, all your time will be spent productively making **'more money from antiques.'**

Incidentally, that's my pet peeve—dealers staring into space or reading a book in their booths. Not only does it look bad, but it certainly doesn't give the customer that comes around the corner confidence in their antiques ability.

Combining the old with the new is a must—so go for it. It'll be fun, and profitable, I promise you.

Proven methods still effective

In introducing these new ways of increasing business, you must not forget what got you here in the first place. Just think about it. In the last three years you went from start-up to a pretty decent antique business, didn't you? So something worked!

What was it? What got you to this stage of development in your thriving antique business? "Mailing lists, flyers, special packaging, follow-up consultations and even short seminars on a Saturday afternoon all built up my clientele," I can hear those attentive readers say! Well done! I'm pleased that some of you are taking notice.

The problem with modern times is that we never seem to have enough hours in the day to get everything done, and so we have to utilize what time we have to do two jobs at once. The web site that took so much money and effort to set up can be printed out and used as flyers. It'll save you having to call up the printer, having to proofread the copy and having to spend more money. That data bank and that colored printer that we now have can do our printing for us. E-mail can be used to place orders, pass messages, and hunt down new antiques. Our accounts which used to take so long to do can now be brought up to date with far less effort, requiring only the data entry—preferably done at the time of purchase or sale—with a few keystrokes. Why, today technology is moving so fast that you can even get hand held computers into which you can enter auction prices, sales details, or descriptions. All these details, entered at the time of the transaction, can be downloaded into your computer by simply connecting the instrument to your PC when you get to your booth or to your home office. And if all this technology is too much for you to cope with, just remember that all you need to know is the basics of how to get what you want done. Any part-time computer school can teach you that in one week.

$ $ $ $ $

Thinking about how proven methods are still effective when combined with new technology, I am always reminded of a TV commercial I sometimes see. In this commercial a major truck manufacturer says, "Let our competitors continue to do it the old way and we will see if they are still around when we are double in size." While stating those words, a background of flashing computer screens is combined with an old-fashioned assembly line behind the executive.

The antiques business, or any business for that matter, is exactly the same. Those that survive and prosper will combine new technology with the proven methods that have worked effectively. Those that don't will have a hard time. Let one of the survivors driving around in a new Jaguar be you!

Changing with the times

The biggest problem all of us encounter when attempting to change with the times is a stubborn mindset. We are all guilty of it, even me. The second problem antique dealers have trouble overcoming is their fear of computers. "I can't understand how they work," some of the older dealers say and I appreciate their hesitancy. I would, however, urge you to overcome this. Using a computer and the Internet is really not that difficult.

My suggestion is this: Find a friend that is already on the Internet and offer to take them out to dinner in exchange for an afternoon's instruction. It will be fun as well as educational. And who knows, the computers that are operated by voice commands will soon be cheap enough for us all to afford. That'll make it easy, won't it? Just speaking at the screen, instead of having to operate the keyboard, sounds like a good idea to me.

One other thing about changing with the times. I have mentioned it before, but **trends** are even more important to your business now than ever. Catch them early to maximize the profits from your antiques business.

Decorating trends

Decorating trends vis-à-vis the antiques business can be boiled down to color, themes, and style. Right now the 'in' colors are dark reds, burnt oranges and the old favorite hunter green. Expect these to stay around for a while. Burgundy is also a favorite.

Themes are nostalgic. That means anything historical. That's

Offer a catalog company a giveaway.

why those 'olde worlde' scenes are so popular. Horses and carriages, pretty ladies with parasols, and cozy fireplace scenes are definitely in.

Style is an easy one, because it has been around for awhile. Rustic is definitely in. It has been growing in popularity during the last three years and I expect it to continue to do so. In addition to rustic, country themes continue as favorites, as does the distressed look. Just don't stock antiques that are too distressed. A little 'distress' is good, too much and it becomes garish.

I hope that the above advice will be a good guide for you, because that's what it is meant to be. I don't profess to be an interior decorator, but when one color starts to crop up time after time, even a dummy like me can deduce that it's the "in" one this year. By the way, don't forget to check out those interior decorating magazines. I know one very successful antique dealer that swears that she lives and dies by them. Observing her success, I think she is onto something.

Breaking out of traditional markets

I have already covered the Internet, but there is a recent trend that seems to hold promise for the aggressive antiques dealer. I can't yet go for it wholeheartedly as it takes effort to organize and you already have enough on your hands, don't you? Anyway, here it is. It's worth watching.

One successful antiques dealer that I know has started holding "Tupperware type" sales both in her house and in her friend's houses. She does this with antique accessories only due to the effort required to set it up, but she claims that it is very successful for her. By holding an "antique" party, she has a captive audience among her friends and acquaintances. It sounds like a good idea to me if you are the aggressive type that doesn't mind mixing your personal and business life. I have even heard of one dealer that does this with furniture, which sounds even more intriguing to me. By setting up a whole room with antique furniture and accessories, the display has tremendous visual effect. Hold a tea party, talk about the different pieces, show them how to display the antiques in their own homes, and you have an almost certain sale. This is an extension of what the interior decorators do. They always show pieces in their customer's home to clinch a commission.

If you decide to try this, and I recommend you do if you can muster up the effort, or if you have willing slave labor such as a pliable husband, don't forget to take your credit card machine with you as well as your receipt book. Just don't go out giving credit to all and sundry. If you do, you are liable to be both embarrassed and poor when you are still chasing payments months later. You will also have lost a lot of friends.

Another way of breaking out of traditional markets that I recommend, is to offer an antique to a catalog company as a giveaway. Obviously it has to be something unusual, but in exchange for it you can ask them for their mailing list. The catalog has got to be one of those specialist ones that sell one-of-a-kind types of items at high prices. I'm sure that you have received an avalanche of them in your mailbox, particularly if you have recently bought an expensive item such as a car or house. This is a good way of enlarging your customer base to a very targeted audience. Now just send out those classy flyers that you set up on your new computer and color printer and you will generate even more business!

Interior decorators

A quick word about working with interior decorators is appropriate here as they are coming into vogue again. It all depends on the economy, you see! When there's lots of money around people want others to do the work for them, when times are tight they do it themselves with much groaning and moaning.

For the antique dealer, working with an interior decorator can be a good partnership. As I said before in *Money from Antiques*, just make sure that everything in your agreement is down in writing so that there can be no misunderstanding down the line.

Money matters can get real messy as we all know.

Hey, I've just had a great thought! How about this?

If you are an aggressive dealer, how about holding an "antiques party" together with your friendly interior decorator at which you can show not just your antiques, but also how to decorate the whole room. Add your carpet suppliers rep, the drapery supplier, and you can show the "whole package."

At that stage you will probably have to hire a ballroom to cater for all your friends, all the interior decorator's customers and friends, and all the carpet company's customers and friends. It could turn out to be quite a shindig! Just let me know how it works out, will you?

Targeting your customers

I'm sure that you are all fully aware that targeting your customer is an important consideration when sending out flyers, but how many of us really give this the thought that it deserves? Not many I bet. And yet, it's our money isn't it?

So how can you tighten up and ensure that your targeted customers are the type that are interested in buying antiques and not just in buying more cosmetics or six packs? Well how about exchanging mailing lists with the carpet supplier that you are now working with, or with the interior decorator's fabric supplier? It's really quite simple. It's called quid pro quo—you scratch my back and I'll scratch yours. It really does save a lot of time and money, believe me. And you get customers that are pre-qualified, having bought a more expensive item than the average Joe.

Targeting your customer also means buying the right merchandise for the income level of the people in the surrounding vacinity of the mall in which your booth is. There's absolutely no point in stocking cheap antiques when your walk-in customer is a professional earning $100,000 a year. The opposite is also true. Expensive antiques will not be bought by working class populations. They don't have that type of disposable income.

In closing this small section I would like to remind you that targeting your solicitations can also mean offering antiques to regular customers at special prices. A handwritten personal letter to the lady that collects antique dolls does wonders in selling the doll that you just bought on the Internet for a song.

 **Checklist**

- ❑ **Combining the new with the old**—redecorate your booth and use the Internet to develop a "worldwide antique locating center."
- ❑ **Proven methods still effective**—don't forget what got you where you're at and keep those mailings, flyers, and seminars going. Customer service is still number one.
- ❑ **Changing with the times**—follow trends such as colors and themes. Overcome your fear of the new technology and get computer literate.
- ❑ **Breaking out of the traditional mold**—hold "antique parties" and offer antiques as special gifts to catalog companies. Build new mailing lists.
- ❑ **Interior decorators**—work with them and other suppliers to expand your customer base. The interior decorating business fits in with yours like a glove.
- ❑ **Targeting customers**—supply targeted customers with specialized antiques to satisfy their requirements. That means sourcing them anyway you can.

Chapter 13

The Nuts and Bolts of the Antiques-Business

In the previous chapters we covered all the new factors affecting the antiques business and how this impacts your future. We also covered how to use these to your advantage. In all the excitement over these new methods of running an antique business we mustn't forget the basics, such as how to tell a genuine antique, how to clean them, how to display product to the best advantage, and how to find the best buys. This is what we are going to cover in this chapter. Let's start with what kind of antiques we should stock in our booth or booths.

What kind of antiques?

When we first discussed what kind of antiques a new dealer should consider when starting out in the business, I advised as follows in *Money from Antiques*: They should be genuine, unusual pieces that can't be found anywhere else. That premise still holds true today. I would also add: antiques that are attractive and useful are the best sellers. In addition, I advised you that you should buy antiques that compliment each other rather than a disparate collection of odd pieces. The reason for this is that you want your booth to be an attractive display. Just as important is the fact that as a professional dealer you should always try to double up on your sales. An example of this is that when selling the antique bed, you have a good chance of selling the matching pair of bedside tables that come with it—as long as you have them. It is unlikely, for example, that the customer would be interested in a dining table when they are focused on re-doing their bedroom.

They should be genuine, unusual antiques that can't be found anywhere else.

However, that full-length mirror that you bought with the bed is a different matter. It is more than likely to go also. It fits into the bedroom.

That's what I mean by displaying complementary items. Beds go with bedside tables, armoires, bedside lamps, and antique rugs. They don't go with a sideboard. In other words, display your antiques as a room grouping to get the best out of your display. I know, I know! That means changing out your booth and pre-planning what kind of display you are going to put in it, doesn't it?

When selling the antique bed, you have a good chance of also selling the bedside tables.

So what kind of antiques should you look for?

How about this. Instead of sticking to one type, i.e. English or French, how about planning months ahead and varying your themes? In one two month period you could display an English dining room with a drawleaf table, oak chairs, buffet, English hunting pictures, and English silverware. The next two months you could go completely rustic and country. Now you will have a scrubbed pine table, six antique cane chairs, a couple of wooden butter churns, an old mangle with its wooden feed-in tray

Go country or rustic with pine.

containing an array of antique spice containers, and even an old dog cart with a large flower decoration on display. Add lots of brightly colored accessories—yellow and sky blue go together really well—and you have a cheerful sunroom ensemble that a customer is liable to buy lock, stock and barrel, so to speak.

"But that means that I have to carry a tremendous amount of inventory," I can already hear a number of the more cautious dealers say. Of course you don't. All you have to do is carry the centerpiece, i.e. the table, chairs, and mangle. Add compatible extras as you sell off the preceding display and in a week your totally new arrangement will be complete. By planning ahead and displaying a room setting, rather than a hodgepodge of items, you will sell matching pieces together, thus doubling your sales.

While writing this I realized what has **really** changed in the antiques business in the three years since I wrote *Money from Antiques*. Now, in 1998 and beyond, all antique dealers are going to have to get more imaginative to be as successful as three years ago. It's not going to be enough just to display products half-heartedly.

Merchandising is going to be the watchword

Think of it like this. As a professional antiques dealer today, you are going to have to be broad-based. Just because you've been buying antiques from your local auctioneer who carries only English antiques is not going to be good enough in the future. You are going to have to utilize the Internet and other suppliers to buy country and rustic, Art deco, Early American and Ethnic antiques. In doing so, your booth will have a completeness that other dealers won't have. Just think, January to March will be the ethnic period, April to June will be country and rustic, July, August and September will be early American, and October to December will be English. That way all the seasons are covered: Ethnic when you are wanting change, country and rustic as spring comes around, early American as you look forward to Thanksgiving, and English as the coziness of winter starts to come upon you.

So I will pose the question again. What kind of antiques? Being the terrific dealer you are, you are going to say "Genuine, unusual, English, ethnic, country and rustic, and Early American antiques to keep customers interested in my booth," aren't you?

Establishing if it's a genuine antique

How to tell if the pieces are really genuine antiques?

As I mentioned earlier, reproductions are flooding the market. They are often so well made that it's difficult to tell the difference from a genuine article. Since this chapter is a review of the nuts and bolts of the antique business, I think that this is a topic that needs re-emphasizing.

Let's start with furniture. Genuine antique furniture has certain giveaways. First is the density of the wood. That old oak or mahogany tree took half a century to grow, not like the rapid growing plantation hybrids of today. This means that the grain is tight and hard. Furniture made out of old oak is very dense and solid. Next we turn to the color and patina of the wood. Old oak, mahogany, or walnut has a patina that is naturally lustrous. It is dark, deep, and filled with a glow. Even old pine looks darker and has more knots than its modern insipid looking counterpart. When polished hard, old timber only gets shinier and more lustrous and does not get dull. Reproduction furniture uses timber which is stained by the manufacturer. Stain comes off if you rub long and hard and will leave residue on the cloth. If you have any doubts about a piece, ask the seller if you can polish the back. Rubbing that chair leg to establish if it is a genuine antique should be no problem to him or her. That means that you should always carry some antique polish and cloths with you, right? I knew you were ahead of me. You're getting good, I'm pleased to say.

$$\$ \ \$ \ \$ \ \$ \ \$$

"But how can I polish the furniture when I buy it at auctions? I can't exactly do that during a pre-showing!"

No, you can't, but you can look into the interior corners, those that are difficult to get at. The Chinese, Thai, or Malaysian worker has to complete the piece in a hurry. It has a ship to catch to America or Europe after all. He, therefore, applies the stain with a wadded cloth which is too bulky to fit into the tight corners. That's what gives a reproduction furniture piece away. The light colored sections in the tight corners where the stain doesn't reach!

The glue and nails used can also be used to identify a genuine antique. Remember those two items? Old antique furniture used bone glue, not the modern chemically mixed ones. You can tell it's old just by looking at it. Bone glue was thick and yellow in color, not clear and hard. The nails and screws were made by hand-operated machines not computer-controlled lathes and often had the slots cut off-center.

And how about accessories? How can we tell if the lamp, ceramic swan, or picture is a genuine antique?

That's much harder—way, way, harder. Look for the markings that all genuine antiques have, ask the piece's history, check around to see if there are any similar pieces in other booths, and look up antique books to establish manufacturer's characteris-

Do you speciaize? Yes, yes, and more yes!

tics. Despite all that, it's getting harder and harder to tell a genuine piece from a fake today. The Far Eastern manufacturers are just too good. They have gotten reproductions down to a fine art. As an example, I will mention something that happened to me.

It was on one of my buying trips in England and I was with another dealer, unfortunately counting on my expertise! Going into a small, dusty, back street antique shop in Swansea, Wales—just the type of location in which you have a good chance of getting a genuine antique at a bargain price—my companion spied some Staffordshire porcelain. Is it genuine? she asked the dealer. "Ov course, luv!" he answered indignantly. "Oi don sell anyfink uv-er den da real ting!" (Excuse my pronunciation but it sounds better in the local accent).

"What do you think?" my companion asked me.

I turned the piece over—it had genuine Staffordshire markings. I peered into the body of the brown and dirty red colored dog—the porcelain was thick, covered with dust and star cracked. I studied the brush marks—they were coarse and almost crude.

Linens are also strong.

"I think so, I think it's a genuine antique," I said in my most convincing tone. Based on that, my dealer friend bought it, as well as the three other pieces that the owner had buried in the back of that dusty, cramped little room in the back streets of Swansea, Wales.

Heck! Those pieces had everything going for them, right?

Three days later we were 60 miles away on the top floor of a Cirencester antique mall.

Right at the back, in another small and cramped, and even dusty booth, there was a whole display of the stuff! Dogs, cats, birds, weasels, badgers, cows, and even sheep—piece after piece of the same porcelain stared me in the face. Red face, I might add! It just goes to show—you can never tell! By the way, after inquiring I found out that the booth was owned by the same gentleman that owned the dusty store in Swansea.

Restoration and things like that

Two years ago I said: "Don't restore antiques." You don't have the time, expertise or ability. That advice is even more true today. If you can't buy it in good condition, don't even consider it. Not unless you already have three helpers and your significant other is getting on your nerves. Don't restore—and don't even think of getting a professional to do it. It costs far too much and you have more important things to do with your time and money. A rule of thumb is that if it was given to you, or you only paid ten dollars for it at that garage sale, then it's worth restoring. After all, you can always get ten dollars for it by sticking it out on the sidewalk only half restored, can't you?

How about doing extra work like fitting in that shelf for the lady wanting to change the armoire into an entertainment center? My answer is yes—as long as it only takes four to six screws and a tube of glue. If it takes a major re-do, forget it. Three years ago I said just the opposite, but then there wasn't as much to do as there is today, was there?

What all this boils down to is this—Is it better to surf the net for that special piece that you can make a lot of money on, or is it better to mount the shelf that will take all day to do?

Now more than ever, an antiques dealer is going to have to use his or her time in the most productive and profitable way possible.

Special items

Do you specialize?

Yes, yes, and more yes! Special items make good profits. As I have mentioned, three years ago I wasn't that enthusiastic about specializing. It only led you to customers that tended to be collectors. Now so many more dealers have entered the antique market that not to specialize will cost you money. By specializing I don't mean turning your whole booth into an egg cup only display, or into a selling only thimbles one. What I mean is that you should take a segment of the market, say antique linens, and turn a sec-

If entering the oriental market, make sure you know what you are doing.

tion of your booth into a specialized corner. Some dealers have gone all the way. One I know is a model train dealer only, but he did this once he had established a large following. Needing the space because his model trains were selling so fast, he was losing money by taking up space with other slower moving items.

If you think that specializing isn't profitable, here's a story that will interest you.

How about specializing in antique windmills? Sound strange? What is even stranger is the fact that the American Wind Power Center and the city of Lubbock, Texas, specializes in antique windmills to the tune of $4.5 million. Yes, Sireeee, that's right! 4.5 million smackaroos! It seems that in 1993, the center and the city bought a collection of 173 windmills from an antiques dealer in the city of Mitchell, Nebraska with $250,000 of hotel and motel revenue. In the following years, they bought more and more of them. Not knowing what to do with antique windmills, they put them into storage. Now however, someone has raised the issue of all that money being spent and in January 1998 the council is due to vote on approval for a National Windmill Project which will use a 28 acre section of the Yellowhouse Canyon Park to house what is believed to be the largest antique windmill collection in the world.

I, for one, think that it's a terrific idea, and if you think that I've made this up, just see the enclosed Associated Press article from the December 18 Fort Worth Star telegram newspaper.

What fascinates me about this story is this. Was one of the 1993 Council Members an antique dealer? Or maybe more than one? And who was it that collected these 173 antique windmills in Mitchell, Nebraska? Lastly, but not least: How did the Lubbock City Council find out about the windmills?

My last thought is this: Someone sure specialized! $4.5 million! Phew!

New antique products that will do well in the future

Wine-related antiques are a sector of the antique business that is doing extremely well. In England, many antique dealers are setting up small wine shops together with their antiques and specializing in the old rare wines as well as ancillary products such as goblets, ice chests, corkscrews, and decanters. This of course requires a liquor license in many states, but if you are prepared to go to this trouble it is worthwhile. The reason that such antique wine shops are doing so well, is that they draw customers from both the wine and the antique buying population. This is definitely a growing segment and highly profitable. One has only to look at the prices of many of these rare wines to understand why. Of course they are not drunk, sir! Most antique wines are used as status symbol decorative pieces. Somehow I find that far more interesting. Just imagine giving your lifelong partner, or friend, a bottle of rare wine together with a beautiful antique ice chest? What could be a better present to show your feelings? Taking pride of place on a mantelpiece, the antique wine bottle would make a really interesting statement of one-upmanship, don't you think? It's also a "savings in a bottle" that will appreciate in value, so to speak.

Another area of the antique business that is doing well is the collectible cigar and cigarette lighter sector.

Those antique Zippo lighters have become extremely valuable. Cigar cutters, ashtrays, lighters, humidors, and a whole plethora of smoker's knickknacks have made this a fast growing segment. It's keeping pace with the upsurge in expensive cigar smoking, I'm told. There was even a segment devoted to this on the Good Morning America TV program just after the 1997 Christmas period.

$ $ $ $ $

Linens are also strong, although these are now getting harder and harder to locate. Antique tablecloths, pillow slips, embroidered sofa covers, and a whole lot more are now causing an upsurge in demand for antique linens.

Chinese and oriental antiques are also very, very big. In many cases really big. That's because the availability of Chinese antiques increased as China began to embrace a free market economy. It's amazing what a bit of money flowing around suddenly does, isn't it?

Sometimes it's not all good though, I'm afraid.

The problem now is that the supply of genuine Chinese antiques has dried up and real products are very difficult to get hold of. Guess what's happening? That's right—reproductions are pouring onto the market! I would caution the average antique dealer as follows: Don't get into Oriental antiques unless you know exactly what you are doing. Even then, be very, very, careful.

Garden antiques, horse-related products, and old antique carpentry tools are also very strong at present. I have already talked about these at length, so I won't cover them again. I will, however, mention that old farm implements are now also in short supply. Old hand-held scythes, wheelbarrows, wooden handled hoes, grain sieves, and even trowels are in demand. I have seen these decorating fireplaces in cozy nooks in restaurants where they give the place an air of rustic bonhomie. I personally like it. One place I know also hangs up sheaves of wheat protected with a coat of clear lacquer among antique milking maids aprons, milking stools, and even the beat up old buckets. Add a few black and white cow pictures and you can almost smell the farm!

This section has been fun. I hope it will help you broaden your specialization ideas.

Just remember my advice—anything farmy is no longer considered old junk, it's now a valuable antique. Buy them for nothing and sell them for a fortune to make even more money from antiques.

Decorating trends

Decorating trends are now coming to rely on antiques more and more. It must be the old weathered look that sets off the garish brashness of modern products. Mind you, they do go together if you know what you are doing. I have a Scottish antique mirror, two African masks, an antique pendulum clock, an art deco gold and green glass mirror, and two modern chrome and deep Burgundy colored lounge chairs all in the same room. Yuck? I think they go well together, so there!

Seriously now. The more decorators use antiques the more business it generates for us all. That can't be bad, can it?

Delivery service

A delivery service is part and parcel of your antique business today. Free delivery within 5 miles and paid delivery of up to 30 miles is the norm. If you don't have a truck, use a for-hire delivery service, or even better, pay a friend $10 to do it for you.

New finishes

The distressed look has become very popular in the last few years. It goes well with the new paints that are on the market. While carrying distressed-look products in your booth or store is a good idea, just make sure they are not ones that are at the extreme end of the scale. For those readers that don't fully understand what distressed means, I would describe it as this: distressed means weather-beaten. Cracks, chips, and dents are okay as long as they are not too deep or too wide.

In the previous chapters I mentioned paints. While this may seem like something that shouldn't concern you, I have already emphasized that antique dealers that make money are involved in all aspects of interior decorating. If you are going to follow their lead you may as well know about some of the new paints coming on to the market.

The most interesting of these is the Ralph Lauren range of paints. Ralph Lauren the clothes designer? Yes, that's right. Now you can see how the trend of offering a whole package can lead to other opportunities related to one's main line of business.

The Ralph Lauren paints are like no others that I know of. The finishes range from the distressed look to a suede finish and even to a velvet one. They are quite fascinating and although pricey, they are selling extremely well. Check them out in your local hardware warehouse. This range of paints fits in with the antique business like a glove.

Another paint finish that is popular is the crackle finish. These can now be bought in spray cans in most hardware and paint outlets. Use them to jazz up your booth. You can also use the verdegris paints that look so good on metal antiques.

New promotion techniques

I have already talked about offering an antique accessory as a prize to catalog companies in exchange for mailing lists and free publicity for your antique business, but there are a whole lot more promotion techniques available to the aggressive new millennium antique dealer. Obviously the Internet is one, both on your own web site, on that of others, and on web sites targeted at the same demographic customers. This gives you a worldwide market. But how about a more localized catchment area? How about using your local paper to attract local business?

One of the first things I did when I started Kings Antiques was to call up my local paper and ask them to do an article on my new business. Since local events are their lifeblood, they quickly sent a reporter and photographer around. You can do the same. The publicity was invaluable and you can duplicate what I did with just one phone call. And how about exchanging flyers with your local carpet wholesaler, hardware outlet, and even the restaurant that used your antiques for decor? You could display their flyers in one small corner of your sales counter in exchange for them doing the same for you. You will be surprised how effective this can be. Most people pick up literature that's free and not forced on them.

Checklist

- ❐ **What kind of antiques?**—Genuine, attractive, useful ones in related collections is what you want.
- ❐ **Is it a genuine antique?**—Dense wood, stains, screws and joints confirm that it is an antique furniture piece. It is much easier to tell if a furniture piece is an antique than if a ceramic item is. History and markings will help to protect you in that case, but only just.
- ❐ **Restoration**—don't do it unless you have a zillion helpers.
- ❐ **Special items**—yes, yes, yes! Specialize by using a corner of your booth. If the antiques that you are specializing in catch on with customers, go with them.
- ❐ **New antique lines**—wine products, garden antiques, Zippo cigar lighters, linens, horse and farm implements, and oriental antiques are hot! Carry at least one or two of these popular product lines.
- ❐ **Decorator trends**—mix-n-match is good as are burnt orange, blood red and hunter green colors.
- ❐ **New finishes**—the distressed look is in—not too distressed—as are the suede and velvet paints. Use them to jazz up your booth.
- ❐ **New promotion techniques**—catalogs, the Internet and the local press all offer new opportunities to advertise your antiques business. Anything that works, goes.
- ❐ **Review**—the basic, well lit, corner booth in a terrifically located mall is still essential to make money. Mix-n-match the basics to the new technology and you have it made in making **more money from antiques**.

Having covered the past I look forward to discussing the future with you in the next chapter. This has been fun, because the antiques business is fun, don't you think?

Chapter 14

$\mathcal{A}$ntiques — a World of Opportunities

For the person thinking about starting an antiques business, the world is full of opportunities. In the three years since I wrote *Money from Antiques*, the antique business has undergone tremendous growth. New opportunities have made it even easier to start your own exciting and diverse business. "I have my own antiques business," brings even more pride than it did before.

One major change, among many changes, will have a significant bearing on your decision to get involved in antiques. While it is true that more start-up funding is required and that costs for a booth in a mall are now much higher, new dealers without sufficient start-up funding, but with just a computer, can start a home based operation. While this is not ideal, it is certainly a possibility. Nothing can replace the immediate cash flow generated from a well-run antiques booth, but failing that, the electronic age has atleast opened new opportunities for a home based operation.

For dealers already established in a thriving mall, your first step in expanding your existing operation must come by opening a second booth. This will give you the capability of rotating stock, of tapping into a different customer base, and of increasing cash flow dramatically. Having said that, being the smart dealer that you are, I am sure that you realize that getting into the electronic age is also a must. The two go hand in hand in today's business climate and you certainly don't want one hand tied behind your back, do you now?

The 10 foot by 10 foot booth will become history.

Imagine this: the antique world is so full of opportunities that 1999 is the start of your new life. Not only will you make **even more money from antiques**, but you will become internationally worldly wise. Won't it be exciting when you switch on your computer and that voice says "You have mail!"? Even more exciting will be the fact that having entered your mail box you see, Auckland, New Zealand; Capetown, South Africa; and Bratislava, Slovakia in the address boxes! Terrific thought, don't you think?

Where are we going?

The antique business will take another giant step forward in the new millennium.

Antique malls will go through continuing transformation. They will become integrated operations and booth holders are going to have to keep up with these fast-paced changes. Not only will antique malls become fully developed entertainment centers, they will even become major ones. Expect to see video arcades and full-service restaurants attached to the bigger, more aggressive malls. Many of them will have over a thousand dealers, booths will no longer be square boxes, but larger retail stores much like in outlet malls, and they will also vary in shape and square footage. In other words, the 10 foot by 10 foot booth will become history. This is because big players will enter the antique business. Once major retailers have antique sections in their own department stores, they will turn their attention to developing their own separate antique retail chains within other people's malls. We are already seeing this with trial units from the Bombay Company, Haverty's furniture stores, and Pier 1 who are carrying more and more nostalgic orientated products.

This trend will in turn spur property developers to build purpose built **antique centers**.

In my area of Grapevine, Texas, a developer is already breaking ground on just such a project. Situated right next to a winery that looks like a medieval country house, this new development is what is termed a 'European shopping village.' It will have cute stores selling unusual merchandise, a park-like atmosphere with cobblestones and trees, it will hold musical events in its "square," and it will be chock full of antique stores. The concept sounds wonderful to me. It will be what every 'Main Street, USA' should be, but is not. It's just a shame that a developer has to build such a purpose built antique center, rather than small country towns doing it with their own dieing main streets.

$$\$ \ \$ \ \$ \ \$ \ \$$$

Successful antique dealers will also operate differently. They will have higher quality antique products, larger areas, be electronically wired with strategically located computers to give directions, and each antique piece will have recorded details and history. The whole retail operation will be decorated to look like an English cottage, an American settler's farmhouse, or a Bavarian rest house.

You're not so sure? Have you seen the new 'Rainforest Cafes' that are causing such a stir in the restaurant business? Serving food is their backbone, but selling merchandise and entertaining the customer is a major part of why they are the fastest growing and most profitable food group around. They make more money on selling merchandise than on selling food, but by combining the two they get the best of both worlds. It's surprising no one thought of it before.

Just look at it like this: not only will the future antique customer be able to buy a wonderful antique tea set in "Ye olde Antique Shoppe," but they will also be able to purchase a London T-shirt, a key chain with an English crest on it, and a small brick paperweight from an English castle. When they are tired, they will sit down and have tea, scones, and cucumber sandwiches in the 1000-seat English tea room. It will of course be set up with small individual garden settings, rather than like a giant impersonal hall.

One more thing. These antique centers will be more than just retail operations. They will have medieval jousting contests, their own auction rooms, and they will even host visiting dealers from around the world in their 'castle' banqueting halls. We might even see a Shakespearean-type hotel attached to the complex and we will definitely see English or Bavarian drinking pubs and fish and chip shops attached.

To summarize: the antique business is going to come of age and become a total antique experience. The customers are demanding it and the business will give it to them.

How will this affect dealers?

Antique dealers will have to come out of their comfort zones. Does this sound too harsh? Just look at many of the booths in your mall. How many of them look like everything is an afterthought with antiques dumped in any corner that happens to be available? That just won't do in the new millennium.

Now, I know that many of my readers will tell me that the problem is their mall and even their town is not developing and is a bit of a backwater. My comment to this is that it's up to you to instigate the changes. Someone has to start them. Why not you? If that is not possible, then my advice is to move out and accept that you will have to drive 20 miles each way to your new booth location. It is the only way to make even more money in the antiques business that you love.

So how do you instigate the changes, as I have advised in the above paragraph? All it takes is a leader. Your mall owners may be tired, they have lived comfortably doing the same thing for years. Why should they change it now? The answer is that if they don't, not only will many dealers go out of business, but you might even start your own major antique center nearby.

In many of the smaller Texas towns that I have visited these past two years, I have noticed such a change coming. Whereas before they had only one big antique mall, they now have several that are all competing and cooperating fiercely.

Competing and cooperating?

Yes. They compete in business, but cooperate in attracting customers interested in a one-stop antique experience. And you know what's surprising about that? You guessed it!

They are all thriving, drawing in more dealers and customers, and even planning to expand as more and more dealers from the surrounding towns jump on the bandwagon and join them!

The other way that the new technology is going to effect the ordinary dealer is that some more aggressive dealers will break away from their booths and become brokers. In doing this, they will contract with dealer groups to locate and buy antiques on a commission basis. They will undertake the payment, transport, and delivery of the products to your booth as a service. It is a business opportunity that is fast developing, and some dealers are already taking advantage of becoming such integrated suppliers.

Antique consultants will also spring up. These experts will contract with the major retailers to do layouts, purchasing, and management projections. Businessmen and businesswomen in suits is what they will become. And why not? The antique business is not just for the elderly. It is also for those younger dealers that want to get on with achieving the American dream!

$ $ $ $ $

Auctioneers will also change. They will have increasing difficulty finding good antiques as the major European suppliers will be selling more of their better products over the Internet through brokers. This will mean that many antique auctions will become more like cheap, secondhand auctions. Dealers that don't anticipate this and establish alternative sources of supply will find that good products will be harder to find. This year I have heard many antique dealers saying: "There wasn't anything good there," when describing the last auction that they attended. Expect that trend to continue.

One final antique activity that will pick up steam is the "antique tour." In the future you will be able to join a buying tour within the United States or overseas. In the last two years, I have developed just such a tour for a major airline. The first pilot tours have taken place and this trend will grow just like the adventure tours have.

How to make money in this new antique environment

I covered most of this in the previous chapters, but have fitted this section in here to offer advice on how a 1999 dealer should operate.

With so much to do, dealers will have to manage their time

more accurately. Saturdays and Sundays will still be taken up with customer service in your booth or booths. Late afternoons during the week will be taken up with managing your Internet operations, running down supplies and updating your web site and product offers. On Thursday evening, you will have to swing past your flyer displays to replenish them before the weekend. Every two months you will have to take out a full day, preferably a Monday, to redecorate and reset your booth. In between all this, you will have to keep an eye on your mail order operation.

Welcome to the new world! You are no longer a part-time dealer. You have a full-time operation going, and now have to become more a business manager than an antique dealer.

That's enough of my yacking. It's time for predictions. This next chapter is where I stick my neck out. Here is this chapter's summary, before I risk all.

 **Checklist**

- ❏ **A world of opportunities**—an antique booth is still the best way to go for immediate cash flow, but if this not possible get into the antiques business via the Internet.
- ❏ **Where are we going?**—malls will become large entertainment centers and "English Villages" will be the norm. Get involved in these new developments if you can.
- ❏ **How will this affect dealers?**—antique dealers will become full-fledged business people. Some will even become consultants. The world is opening up, so seize whatever opportunity presents itself.
- ❏ **How to make even more money from antiques**—dealers will set up total operations and become fully integrated with interior decorators, carpet suppliers, and even house painting companies.

We are coming to the end of this book. The last chapter will deal with my predictions for the future. It should be fun because the ones in the first book, *Money from Antiques*, weren't bad. Let's go for it together!

redictions

Is this really the last chapter? I can't believe it. I hope it has been as much fun for you to read this book as it has been for me to write it. Because it's the last chapter, I am going to make a number of predictions and offer some encouragement for both those established dealers and those new people considering the antiques business.

The antique business is still a business for anyone with a minimum amount to invest and the desire to succeed. As it was three years ago, the very nature of how the antique business operates allows anyone with a desire to be their own boss to earn sufficient income to live comfortably and even become well off. The advent of the antique malls five years ago was the key. Without the worry of long term leases at high rental, the risk for the average person was acceptable.

This is going to change in the near future. It will have both a positive and negative effect on the antiques business.

Predictions

Antique malls—Three years ago I wrote in *Money from Antiques*, as many readers will remember, that antique malls had come about as a result of landlords having large retail premises going empty. "I rent it out in smaller booths to multiple tenants since I can't find one large customer," a landlord told me. That premise still holds true today. The fundamental change is that whereas five years ago landlords did that out of desperation, today they follow that policy to maximize profits, rather than to cover expenses.

One other change affecting antique malls, is that there has been a shake-out in the number that are around. Many have closed as a result of being in bad locations, and due to the fact that they didn't become entertainment centers as well as antique retail operations. This has left more booth holders requiring space in better organized malls.

The antiques world is at your feet.   *(London)*

As a result, rents are going up and malls charge up to seven percent of sales for ancillary services. That has put up the costs of starting an antique business, as well as the prices of the better quality antiques now necessary to succeed in the new climate.

In addition, larger players have entered the antique market. The net effect of this is that landlords use them as 'anchor' tenants in their malls to cover overheads. So where does the landlord make the profit? You guessed it! From the booth holders taking up the rest of the space. After all, the demand is in that segment of the mall, isn't it?

Think of it this way.

The "Grandma's Antique" mall has 200,000 square feet of retail space. It rents out 75,000 of that to one large tenant. This rental covers 75% of the basic costs of running the mall. Now the landlord can breathe easier. To make up the 25% deficit and to make a profit, he has to charge higher rent per square foot for the rest of the 125,000 square feet. Since tenant demand for smaller booths is high, he will maximize this and therefore, single booth holders will see their rents rising in increments every six months at least. It's unfair I know, but that's how it operates. Supply and demand is the name of the game.

But all is not gloom and doom. Many dealers are now established and forced into making a decision on expanding or folding, they will expand and thus become 'anchor' tenants themselves.

So my predictions for 1998 and beyond are as follows.

Successful antique dealers will become even more successful. To do so, they will become more businessmen and women than antique dealers. Malls will also become full-fledged retail businesses, instead of being just real estate holdings struggling to cover costs. This success will be seen by developers looking for an edge. They in turn will develop a purpose-built 'antique center' to cater for the pent-up demand. The result being that the small antique dealer will need more financial backing to start and develop his or her business, particularly due to the higher costs of rental space and quality antique pieces. The market for these will tighten up and establishing sources of reliable supply will be vital. That isn't all bad.

$ $ $ $ $

As the antique business comes of age, so it will be easier to borrow start-up capital. An antique business will no longer be thought of by lending institutions as a 'rag and bones' business, but as a genuine retail operation with the same pluses and minuses as any stationer, card shop, or traditional gift store. That can't be all bad now, can it? No longer will the antique dealer get the bum's rush when applying for a loan, which was what happened in the past. At least now we will be treated equally by the lending institutions—the banks in particular.

It will mean, however, that running your antique business by the seat of your pants will no longer be enough. Dealers will have to be far more professional in their approach, in their planning, and in their control of costs and operations. Financial institutions will demand it. Asset statements, profit and loss projections, and monthly income statements will be vital. Dealers will know in which direction their businesses are going and what is happening on a month to month, if not week to week, basis. This will be made easier by the new technology whereby accounts can be produced with just a few keystrokes. That is as long as the data is entered, of course!

New technology will have a double effect on the antique business. On the one hand, it will allow the established dealer to operate more efficiently and accurately, while at the same time, it will relieve some of the chores. Pressing a computer key to establish the bottom line cannot be that bad, can it? If you hate the boring and time consuming chore of adding up rows of figures, the new accounting programs that do this for you are a heaven-sent boon.

New technology will also open up the antiques world (as opposed to area) to the serious dealer. The Internet, E-mail, the ability to transmit images worldwide, and the opening of new supply lines and buyer inquiries is an earth shattering development. In three short years an antique dealer is no longer just dependent on walk-in traffic and local promotions. Wow! This sure has been a quantum leap!

$ $ $ $ $

New dealers starting out need not be left behind, not unless they can't, or won't, cope with all these technological changes. The same goes for older dealers. If dealers cannot afford to open, or maintain, a booth in a super 'antique center' they will be able to become an antiques dealer using just their Hewlett Packard, Acer, Gateway or Macintosh, and operate from their front room. This won't be as cash flow productive from the 'get go' but it will at least be a start.

So where will all this electronic wizardry take the antique business in the future?

How about a dealer being able to bid on auctioned items anywhere in the world? No longer restricted to having to have a physical presence, auctions will become worldwide electronic affairs. A dealer in Iola, Wisconsin will be able to bid on a porcelain plate being auctioned in New York, Dallas, or Manchester, England, just as easily as if they were there. All one will have to do is switch on your computer, connect to the auction house, and watch as the items are featured and bidding commences. Pressing a key will send your bid in instantaneously. This will be flashed on a large screen behind and in front of the auctioneer as the physical bidding continues apace. An electronic payment, instant confirmation of receipt, one week for delivery and a quick 'clean-up' later and the plate will be on show in your booth with the sign "Direct from England" proudly displayed. You will of course have to instruct your computer to wake you up at one a.m. You want to be alert when the bidding starts, don't you? Oh, and did your computer tell you that the time difference between Dallas and Manchester was six hours? If on the other hand you are just too lazy to wake up, you will have to instruct it to send in your silent bid as soon as the bidding gets to $50 dollars below what you want to pay for that plate. All this will be done by **talking** to your work station instead of having to type on the keyboard! Amazing, isn't it?

Time and management

Predictions are all very well, but how are you going to cope with all this work? It's getting to be far too much as it is, even with all the electronic wizardry! There just aren't enough hours in the day to do everything.

Which brings me to my next prediction.

The antique dealer will become a part-time employer. Remember that girl friend that is a homemaker because she has three small kids? Well, she'll do your computer entries for you. All you will do is scan the receipts, sales slips, telephone bills and check stubs into your data base, transmit them with a few key strokes to her computer, she will enter them, get totals and balances, hit a key, and bingo! Your accounts are up to date. Now it's up to you to send an 'electronic payment transfer' for her 'services rendered' into her account!

Let's take my predictions even further. Just imagine this: You have a new Mercedes in the three-car garage. It's parked next to the red Porsche Boxter. The last space is empty because your better half is using the cute, new VW bug today.

Sitting in front of three networking screens, you sip your coffee as you switch from each of your three antique locations to your sales totals, to your Internet inquiries, to the auction going on in Cardiff, Wales. You really must tell Linda, who works part-time for you in booth number three, that the brass framed mirror needs polishing! It's obvious even from the camera image being transferred through your computer.

Next you turn your attention to accounts.

Having bought the crystal vase at the auction, you punch the sales receipt into the electronic purchases folder so that your homemaker friend will download it when she totals up sales figures later that afternoon. What a shame you missed out on that sealed bid for that chatelaine at the auction in Houston! You really wanted that and would have gone the extra $100. Oh, you actually got it? How could you have forgotten that you had electronically triggered a second bid when the item reached $600? It'll suit that lady in Helsinki, Norway perfectly. Now all you have to do is send her the image electronically and ask her to transmit the payment before shipping it out tomorrow.

Sitting back, you take another sip of your coffee. "When was it that I actually saw one of my antique pieces last?" you wonder.

Anticipating the Future

I, for one, anticipate the future. I think that with the solid basis that the business has plenty of product still available, although more expensive, a more professional approach by antique malls, and an easily accessible worldwide market—the antique business is poised for even a larger expansion than we have seen in the last five years. Money can definitely be made in this business, we are all just going to have to be more open minded, adventurous, and hard working.

Going for it!

For all those readers still procrastinating about getting involved in the antiques business, I say, "Go for it!" Times are even more conducive to opening your own operation. Opportunities abound, from getting involved on the Internet to opening a large retail operation. If you can afford the start-up costs, now about $15,000, then starting with a booth in an antique mall is still the way to go. If not, start trading electronically until you have enough start-up funding built up to open a traditional booth.

For established dealers, I would also say, "Go for it!" Now is the time to expand, whether into a single larger operation, into a multiple booth operation, or even into a large retail outlet. Unlike the beginner however, you have far more to do. You will definitely need help and I would recommend that you hire part time people to assist you. The bookkeeper I mentioned previously is a start. Electronic technology will be essential and it will both expand your antiques business as well as help you manage it more successfully, and therefore more profitably.

In closing, I wish all the people involved in the antiques business the greatest of success, and even more money from the antiques business. You are a wonderful group of people and it is a pleasure to be involved with you.

I bid you peace.

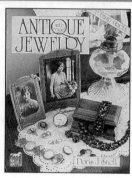